Life Issues

A CHRISTIAN PERSPECTIVE

CHRIS WRIGHT

A LION BOOK

Does it matter?

● ●

This book is about ISSUES which matter in today's world. What do you think are the important issues today?

Does It Matter?

Every day children and grown-ups die
from hunger and thirst.
Does it matter?
We say while we vomit
to stay thin.

Every day, people are shot and
killed in war.
Does it matter?
We say while shooting each other
with our toy guns.

Every day animals are killed
for science.
Does it matter?
We say as we smear lipstick
on our mouths to look beautiful.

Every day the ozone layer
gets thinner.
Does it matter?
We say while spraying ourselves
with deodorant and perfume.

Every day trees are
chopped down in the rain forest.
Does it matter?
We say while tossing out the paper
we just used.

Every day there are children
unable to get an education.
Does it matter?
We say while claiming to have a sore throat
in order to skip school.

Every day there seems to be
a little less of this world.
Does it matter?

Benedicte Fikseaunet, 14, Norway
(From *A World in Our Hands*, Tricyle Press, Peace Child International)

❏ **Make up your own poem entitled 'Does It Matter?'**

Contents

What's Right, What's Wrong?

Dead right

Great idea!

NO WAY!

Good Move

WRONG!

Over my dead body

❏ Is war right
(a) always
(b) sometimes
(c) never?

❏ Why do people differ in their opinions on what is right and wrong on this issue?

❏ **Do you say things like this?**

❏ **Do you believe some things are right… and others wrong?**

❏ **Where do people get their ideas of right and wrong from?**

We all live in the same world, but we don't all see it in the same way. What one person thinks is right is counted as wrong by another. One reason for this is because we all think different things are important. We have different beliefs.

When we use words like 'right' and 'wrong' we are using moral language. The word 'morality' refers to what is right and wrong behaviour.

❏ **What is happening in this photograph?**

❏ **Do people agree on what is right and wrong in this situation? Explain why.**

❏ **What do you think about this issue?**

Introducing the Christian world view

Our views of right and wrong are like spectacles—they affect the way we see the world.

About a third of the world's population call themselves Christians. This book will help you to see the world as a Christian sees it. It will help you to try on the Christian 'spectacles' by introducing you to how Christians work out their morality—their ideas of what is right and what is wrong. It is not asking you to believe in these things. This book simply asks you to take some time to understand Christian points of view.

In order to help you the book has been split

Our views of right and wrong are like spectacles —they affect the way we see the world. How does the Christian viewpoint of the world compare with your own?

into four sections. The first section explains how Christians work out their morality. It looks at such questions as:

❏ **Why do Christians base their morality on what God wants?**

❏ **Who is God anyway?**

❏ **How do people know what God's standards are?**

❏ **What happens if people fall short of God's standards?**

The last three sections look at how Christian morality applies to different issues: personal (units 14–28), world issues (units 29–41) and what it says about the future (units 42–44).

SUMMARY
This page looks at issues of morality—of what is right and what is wrong. Now you are going to be looking at what Christians believe is right and wrong.

T h e Godzone

MY PLACE

❑ Do you have a place which you can call your own?

❑ How do you show that you 'rule' in your room? How is your room different from any other in the house?

I RULE-OK

What message are these signs giving?

In some places special rules apply. Christians use the image of a great ruler to describe God. Where God rules is referred to as God's Kingdom. One writer calls it 'The Godzone'.

Godzone is different. As far as I'm aware, there are no signs indicating where it starts and stops. I have never seen a sign declaring, 'You Are Now Entering Godzone'. And for good reason. *You never do enter it, or leave it for that matter. Wherever you are, you're in Godzone. It is not a place at all, in the strict sense of the word. It's the space inhabited by God. Even though you never cross the borders, there is a certain knack to seeing it. It's not immediately obvious.* Some people don't believe it exists. Some people don't believe in God.

Michael Riddell, *Godzone*, Lion Publishing

66 I believe that God is the Creator and therefore King of the whole universe. God created the world and said it was good. It is still God's world whether people recognize God or not. **99**

Anton, 14

If you love someone, you want to please them. Christians want to do what pleases God.

Living in Godzone

Christians believe that people are able to accept God as the king of their life in a very real way. God enters into a friendship with them. They can learn more and more about how God loves them and accepts them. They want to respond by returning God's love and loving other people. In the Bible there are the terms of an agreement people believe God

This is one image of creation by William Blake. What words would you use to describe the way Blake has painted God? How has the artist tried to portray God in relation to the human?

BRAIN ENGAGE

1 Why do you think Michael Riddell refers to the Kingdom of God as the Godzone? What do you think he means in the italicized words?

2 What things are important in the world? Look through magazines and look at adverts on television. Make a montage of magazine clippings which illustrate what things are important in the world—what really rules people's lives.

3 Commandments 1–4 deal with putting God first in life. How do people act when they put another person 'first' in their life—someone they have fallen in love with, for example? What clues does this provide for how people might put God first?

4 Look through a newspaper. Find examples of ways in which people have ignored commandments 5–10, and say how their action has hurt other people. Make a montage of your findings.

✔ You must not steal.

✔ You must not tell lies to get people into trouble.

✔ You must not envy what others have, wanting it for yourself.

gave them, which spell out what it means to respond to God's love. One summary of these terms is the Ten Commandments.

They can be divided into two groups. First, how to love God:

✔ Worship no god but God.

✔ Do not worship anything else—trust only in God.

✔ Respect God's name.

✔ Keep one day in seven as a day for God—a day of rest from work.

Second, how to love other people:

✔ Respect your father and mother.

✔ You must not commit murder.

✔ You must not commit adultery.

At the heart of the agreement is a promise to put God first in everything you do.

❝ When you think of Christianity what image comes to mind? Some people think of a long list of dos and don'ts, with more don'ts than dos. 'If it's fun, then don't do it.' But this is to misunderstand why God gave us his commands. He gave them to show us how to respond to his love. The law of God is a bit like the laws of health—the law of your own happiness. ❞

Richard

SUMMARY
• • • • • • • • • • • •
Christians believe that God is King of the universe and a God of love. They want to respond to that love by entering into an agreement with God.

The Drop-dead Look

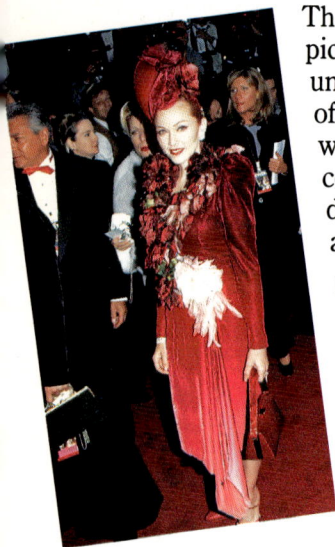

The last page looked at one picture of God—as ruler of the universe and, potentially, king of a person's life. But who or what is God? This page considers two more descriptions of God—as holy and as a lover.

❑ **What elements in this photograph tell you that the person is a 'star'?**

❑ **Why do you think we call some famous people 'stars'?**

❑ **What feelings do you have about your favourite 'stars'?**

Human 'stars' are often described as glamorous. They appear to live lives which are far removed from everyday things. When they appear in public, they have that 'drop-dead look' which makes ordinary people feel overawed—star-struck!

This image of a human 'star' gives a clue to understanding a word which is often used to describe God—'holy'. By this the Bible authors meant that God is greater than humans. God is above anything people know. God is pictured surrounded by mystery which makes people hold their breath. People take great care when approaching God in worship; they show respect.

❑ **Why do you think people get excited when they see that it has snowed during the night?**

❑ **What other feelings does freshly-fallen snow create?**

God is holy

The way people feel when they see the perfect beauty of freshly-fallen snow is just a hint of how Christians feel when they think of God's perfect goodness—God's holiness.

The word 'holy' describes God's perfect nature. Christians believe that God made people and God wants them to be holy too, and that's why God has said that there is a right way to live. God has set holy standards, not to make life miserable and hard but to allow love and happiness to grow. The Christian way of life is called holiness.

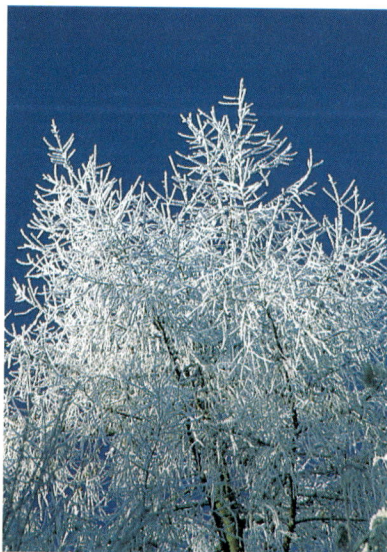

❑ **What do Christians mean when they say that God is holy? How has the artist in the painting on the right tried to show the holiness of God—what symbols have been used, what colours? Imagine that you saw this painting on holiday in an art gallery. Write a postcard home describing it.**

God is a lover

❑ **How many of you have received a valentine card? What do you think about them?**

The Bible says 'God is love.' (1 John 4:8) The Bible often describes God as a faithful lover. Picture this:

❑ **What would you think if God told you to go and marry a prostitute?**

❑ **What would you think of a man who remained faithful to**

Three ways of understanding God—as Father, Son and Holy Spirit.

his wife even when she returned to her old job as a prostitute, or a woman who remained faithful to her unfaithful husband?

Although this might sound highly unlikely, it is exactly what happened to a man named Hosea whose story is told in the Bible. His wife Gomer was a prostitute but God wanted Hosea to love her. Gomer continued to be unfaithful to Hosea and hurt him very much, but Hosea never stopped loving and forgiving his wife. Christians believe that this is like a picture of the way God loves people: God loves people despite the fact that they are unfaithful. (Hosea 3:1)

66 **Because God loves me whatever I do, I am called to love other people.** 99

Jessica, 18

BRAIN ENGAGE

4 Imagine you are Hosea and that your best friend knows Gomer is being unfaithful. Write to him, explaining why you still love her and do not regret marrying her.

5 How is God's love different from human love? Look up Romans 5:8 to help you.

SUMMARY
. . . .
Christians believe in a holy God who sets holy standards for people to live by. They also believe that God loves people for who they are, even when they fail to live up to these standards.

9

Rebellion

KRISTEN'S DIARY

3 MAY

Stayed out till 11.30 last night. Mum and Dad went mad when I returned home. All I wanted to do was to sneak upstairs and go to bed. But they had purposely waited up, only to 'have it out with me once and for all'. Why won't they let me grow up? I'm sixteen—old enough to look after myself.

18 MAY

Got drunk last night—I had to do something to forget about life at home—it's one continuous row with Mum. Why don't parents try to understand? It's getting worse—it makes me want to pack my bags and get out of here. I can't stand it much longer.

24 MAY

John's phoned. I told Mum and Dad—they exploded: they're trying to control who I see now. All they do is go on at me—at least John loves me.

7 JUNE

Things have come to a head. Dad's found out I smoke drugs. I tried to explain it was all harmless stuff but he lost his rag and has grounded me for two weeks. I hate them—I feel trapped in a prison. I'm going to have to escape.

11 JUNE

I've finally done it—I've escaped. John said I could move in with him—it's hello to a free life.

20 JULY

It wasn't supposed to turn out this way. John was so loving before but I never saw him so angry as last night. The left side of my face is swollen, I can hardly eat a thing. What can I do?

The great rift

Kristen's diary describes rebellion from the point of view of a teenager. Rebellion is a central theme in the Bible.

At the beginning of the Bible you will find the story of Adam and Eve. In the story, God created these people and gave them the choice of how they lived their lives. The story is set in a garden where everything is perfect and where everything is created for their enjoyment. There is only one thing which they have been forbidden to eat.

One day, when Eve was alone, a serpent came and spoke to her.

'Why don't you eat the fruit of that tree in the centre of the garden?' it asked.

'God has told us not to,' Eve replied. 'We must not eat it; we must not touch it. If we do, we will die.'

'Oh, no, no,' said the serpent. 'That's simply not true. Let me tell you why God has forbidden you to eat it…' And lowering its voice, it hissed, 'God knows that if you eat it, you will be like God, knowing both good and bad. Imagine… you will be as wise as God.'

Eve thought about that. Wise… like God. So she selected a piece of fruit. She plucked it down from the tree. And she ate it.

Immediately she wanted her companion Adam

to be like her. So she gave him some to eat too. And then everything changed. They did have understanding. They realized first of all that they were naked, so they made clothes to cover themselves. And that evening, God came as usual to talk with them. They knew they had done what God had forbidden, so they hid from him.

The perfect relationship they had with God and with nature was shattered. Guilt and fear crept into their relationship with God. They were sent out of the garden and wandered in a wilderness of their own making.

People understand this story in different ways:

66 **There was a place called the Garden of Eden, and there was a man called Adam.** 99

Rebecca, 17

66 **The story is a myth which explains the relationship between God and humankind and how it has gone wrong; why we are not so close to God.** 99

Philip, 15

66 **This story captures a basic truth—that all people turn away from God.** 99

Tim, 18

BRAIN ENGAGE

4a Read through the extract from the Bible story again. What feelings do you think the woman has in this story? What might she be thinking?

4b Parents often cry over their child who insists on going their own way. What feelings might God have in this story?

5 How does life change once God finds people hiding from him? How does Adam and Eve's relationship with God change? Read the rest of Genesis chapter 3 to find out. Act out this story in mime.

6a What do you think is the point in the story when things start to change?

6b Which part of the story does the painting by Rousseau illustrate? Why do you think he has given the painting the title *The Snake Charmer*?

6c Sketch your own scene from this story bringing out the turning point in the story.

7 Write a modern story in which the themes of the rebellion of Adam and Eve are expressed.

The Snake Charmer by Henri Rousseau. What is 'paradise' like in this picture? What is your idea of paradise?

SUMMARY
The Bible tells the story of how people have rebelled against God.

Lost!

❑ **Have you ever felt lost? What did it feel like? What happened?**

❑ **What might be going through this young person's mind?**

People can be lost in different ways. Sometimes it is a physical lostness, like being lost in a place you have never been to before. Sometimes it is emotional loss, when you are feeling hurt and betrayed, or feel that no one loves you.

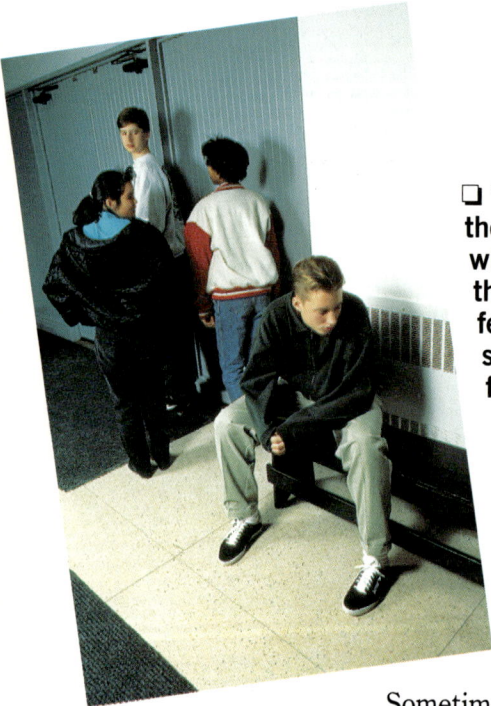

❑ **What might the person who is outside this group feel? In what sense is he feeling lost?**

❑ **Have you ever felt like this?**

Sometimes people have a feeling of being spiritually lost, of not knowing what life is all about; which way to go in life. It is at these times, amongst others, that people cry out 'What's the purpose of life?', 'Where am I going to?'

A compass can help you find your bearings if you are lost.

Far from God

Christians sometimes use this image of 'being lost' to talk about their relationship with God. God feels far away, and silent. The following prayer was written by King David in the middle of war. He was one of the great Jewish kings mentioned in the Old Testament. Although he believes in God, he feels that God is a long way from him—he has lost sight of God.

How much longer will you forget me, Lord? For ever?
How much longer will you hide yourself from me?
How long must I endure trouble?
How long will sorrow fill my heart day and night?
How long will my enemies triumph over me?

Psalm 13:1–2

❑ **What feelings does David have in the poem above? What does he feel about God? In what sense is he lost?**

BRAIN ENGAGE

1 Draw an illustration or picture to represent a feeling of being lost.

2 People sometimes talk about a loss of innocence—when someone does something wrong. Describe a time when you have done something wrong which made you feel frightened of being found out. What did it feel like?

3 Either watch the news on television or search through a recent newspaper. Write down all the different news stories which talked about people being lost (e.g. refugees, personal stories of people trapped in conflict with each other). Share these with the class. Draw a table with three columns for: physically lost; emotionally lost; spiritually lost. Fill in the stories under each column.

4a What kinds of help do people need in the following situations?

♦ When they lose their way on a car journey.

♦ When they are lost on a mountainside in dense fog.

♦ When they have lost their best friend.

♦ When they have lost the meaning for living.

♦ When they feel that God is far away from them.

4b Suggest ways in which people could find ways out of their lostness.

What feelings is this woman experiencing? Why might she feel lost or far from God?

SUMMARY
Christians believe that there is a rift between God and people. As a result, people feel lost at times.

13

The Moral Maze

❑ **Have you ever been in a maze? What does it feel like?**

It is very easy to get lost in good mazes: people can spend hours trying to find their way out. Human life can be compared to a maze—a moral maze—in which people have to work out how to act in any given situation.

Some mazes, like the wooden one in the picture, operate by means of a mechanism which tilts the board so the player can roll the metal ball along it. If this mechanism didn't work properly, it would mean that the player would be bound to lose—the metal ball would always fall down the trap-holes in the board causing the player to start the game all over again.

Christians believe that human life is like a moral maze in which people have free choice to make their own decisions on how to act. But it is as if the 'mechanism' to steer us out of trouble has got stuck. People can see the right direction—living in a way that is loving, forgiving, healing and helping. Many admire those who live in this way. Yet most find themselves rolling down into a hole instead—they are only interested in taking care of themselves regardless of the effect on others. Christians describe this tendency to fall short of God's holy standards as 'sin'.

In the Bible, a Christian named Paul put it this way:

I do not understand the things I do. I do not do what I want to do, and I do the things I hate.

Romans 7:15

❑ **Think of a situation where you have said or done things you regret. Do you think you would act differently another time?**

Sometimes people become addicted to negative ways of acting, as in the case of Judith.

JUDITH: CASE STUDY

Judith started misusing alcohol when she was at college. By the time she was in her early twenties she was an alcoholic. She went on to get married and have two children but her drinking habits remained the same. 'So long as I could keep down a job and bring up the children I felt I had everything under control.' Then things started to go wrong—the fights with her husband, then the divorce and a child who nearly died from fever. Judith started to drink more and more—for comfort and sometimes to forget. 'The worse I felt about myself,' she said, 'the more I drank. In the end I wanted to die. So for six solid days I drank.' Judith ended up in a hospital bed. 'I lay there and I cried. I couldn't even kill myself properly.'

Adapted from 'Not Alone…', *Youth Bible*, Word Publishing

BRAIN ENGAGE

1a Judith became addicted to alcohol. What other things do people become addicted to?

1b What reasons does Judith give for becoming addicted? Look carefully at the passage to find out why she took alcohol.

1c How is Judith's addiction like the 'inner battle' which Paul describes going on within him?

2 Watch an hour of television. Jot down all the moral decisions which people have to make. Write it up in the form of a report entitled 'The Moral Maze'.

The following story illustrates the effect of sin upon a person.

The two faces of Pietro

When Leonardo da Vinci was painting his masterpiece *The Last Supper* he looked for a model for his drawing of Christ. He finally chose a beautiful young man called Pietro Bandinelli.

Years passed and the painting remained unfinished. Leonardo had painted all the disciples except Judas Iscariot, the man who betrayed Jesus. He wanted to find a man to sit for his painting of Judas whose face was hardened and distorted by sin. At last he found a beggar on the streets of Rome: he had a face like a criminal. Leonardo hired him. When he had finished the painting of Judas and was about to send the man away he said, 'I have not yet found out your name.'

'I am Pietro Bandinelli,' he replied. 'I also sat for you as your model of Christ.'

Adapted from *Assemblies for School Children's Church* by R.H. Lloyd, The Religious and Moral Education Press

Pietro's life had been eaten away by sin.

BRAIN ENGAGE

3a Can you tell anything about a person's character by looking at their face?

3b How had Pietro's face changed?

3c What do you think Leonardo was looking for when he wanted a man whose face was distorted by sin—what do you think he would look like?

4 Sin has been described as a cancer which takes over the whole person unless cured. It can also be likened to ivy which can choke a plant unless it is torn down. Draw your own picture to illustrate sin. Give it a title.

The Last Supper by Leonardo da Vinci. Can you imagine what the people might be saying?

SUMMARY

Christians believe that God created people with the freedom to choose between a God-centred life and a self-centred life. People are caught in a moral maze. However, people have a bias to live a self-centred life.

THURSDAY 13TH FEBRUARY 1997

Five Men Trapped In Collapsed Mine

Five men remain trapped 1000 metres underground after a mine shaft collapsed last night. Rescue teams have been working all night to locate the men and make an escape route secure. There is only one way out of the mine—all other routes collapsed under the force of the explosion. It could be hours before all men are free. The rescue team themselves know that conditions underground are far from secure. They risk being killed along with the miners.

FRIDAY 14TH FEBRUARY 1997

Man Loses Life On Rescue Mission

At 2.15 a.m. this morning fireman Sam Fellowes died after he was crushed by an avalanche of rock. He was part of one of the rescue teams sent to save the miners. Two miners still remain underground.

BRAIN ENGAGE

1 What personal qualities do you think a member of the rescue team would possess?

2 In the newspaper story it was a fireman who died in his attempt to help the miners. Which other groups of people risk their lives to help others?

3 Write a story of a rescue mission bringing out the possible cost for the rescuer.

4 Read the story of Zacchaeus. In what sense was he rescued? Imagine that you are Zacchaeus. Write a diary account of your meeting with Jesus. Record your feelings before and after the meeting.

Jesus the rescuer

In Hebrew 'Jesus' means 'God rescues'. Christians believe that God sent Jesus on a rescue mission to show people the way back to God.

Jesus told a number of other stories to bring the point home that he had come as God's rescuer to seek and save the lost. He told a story about a shepherd who had one lost sheep—and who went out looking for it. (Luke 15:3–7) He described himself as 'the Good Shepherd'. Another story was about a woman who had lost a coin in her house—and who turned the place upside down until she found it. (Luke 15:8–10)

In the same way, Christians believe that God loves people so much that he makes the first move to find those who feel lost.

Christians believe that Jesus showed people how to live in the right way—accepting and befriending people who others had rejected and risking his health and reputation in doing so. He was tireless in doing good—helping, healing, getting on with dull chores while his followers argued about which of them was the greatest. He told people of God's love, knowing that many felt he had no right to be a religious leader. His enemies were so enraged at his teaching about God that they arranged to have him put to death on trumped-up charges.

To save the lost was a costly rescue mission—one that cost him his life. But even at the end of his life, Jesus showed that he had come to save even his enemies. He prayed aloud for the people who were crucifying him saying, 'Father, forgive them, for they know not what they do.'

A man named Zacchaeus was one such 'lost' person. When Jesus met him, something dramatic happened.

Zacchaeus

Narrator: Zacchaeus was a very unpopular man—he was a tax collector who worked for the Romans and he had become very rich.

When Jesus entered Jericho, Zacchaeus ran ahead and climbed a sycamore tree so that he could see him better above the crowds. As Jesus passed by the tree, he looked up.

Jesus: Come down Zacchaeus! I must stay in your house tonight. Hurry!

Narrator: Zacchaeus was amazed and welcomed him joyfully, but all the people who heard this started grumbling.

Grumbler: Can you believe it! He's going as a guest to the home of a sinner!

Narrator: But Zacchaeus stood up and said…

Zacchaeus: Sir, listen to me! I will give half my possessions to the poor and if I have cheated anyone, I promise I'll pay them back four times as much.

Jesus: Salvation has come to this house today… The Son of Man came to seek and save the lost.

Luke 19:1–10

Safe at last

Christians believe that Jesus' rescue mission was successful beyond all imagining. True, he lost his life in the process. But his followers at the time firmly believed they saw him alive again—that God had raised him to new life. They believed that to follow Jesus was just as risky—and just as safe in the end!

Rescuers risk their lives for people they have never met. Christians believe Jesus went even further and knowingly accepted death for the sake of others.

SUMMARY
• • • • • • • • • • • • •
Christians believe that Jesus was sent by God on a rescue mission to free (save) people from the control of sin and to show them the way back to God. His teaching was radical.

A Call to Faith

❑ **What thoughts and feelings do you have as you look at this photo?**

❑ **What thoughts and feelings might the person in the photograph be having? Why do you think they are doing this?**

❑ **What personal qualities does the person have to do this?**

One quality which this person has is faith. To have faith means to trust, to rely on something or somebody. It involves action and can involve risks.

❑ **What or whom is the person in the photograph having faith in?**

❑ **In what ways is he showing that faith can involve taking risks?**

A story is told of a great explorer who returned home. His friends were eager to learn about his adventures and especially about the mighty Amazon. All night he shared his excitement at the wild animals, the beautiful flowers, the smells and sounds of the forest and the danger of the rapids.

At the end he said to the people, 'Go and find out for yourselves.' To help them he drew a map of the river. They fell upon the map, framed it and hung it in their town hall. As they studied it they became experts in understanding the river—they knew its every turn and where every rapid and waterfall were. And yet not one of them ever left the village to go and see for themselves.

Michael Riddell, *Godzone*, Lion Publishing

BRAIN ENGAGE

1 In what ways did the explorer differ from the people in his village? How did the explorer show faith?

2 Why do you think the villagers framed and studied the map instead of exploring the Amazon for themselves? What were they missing out on? Do you think they thought they were missing out? In what way did they not show faith?

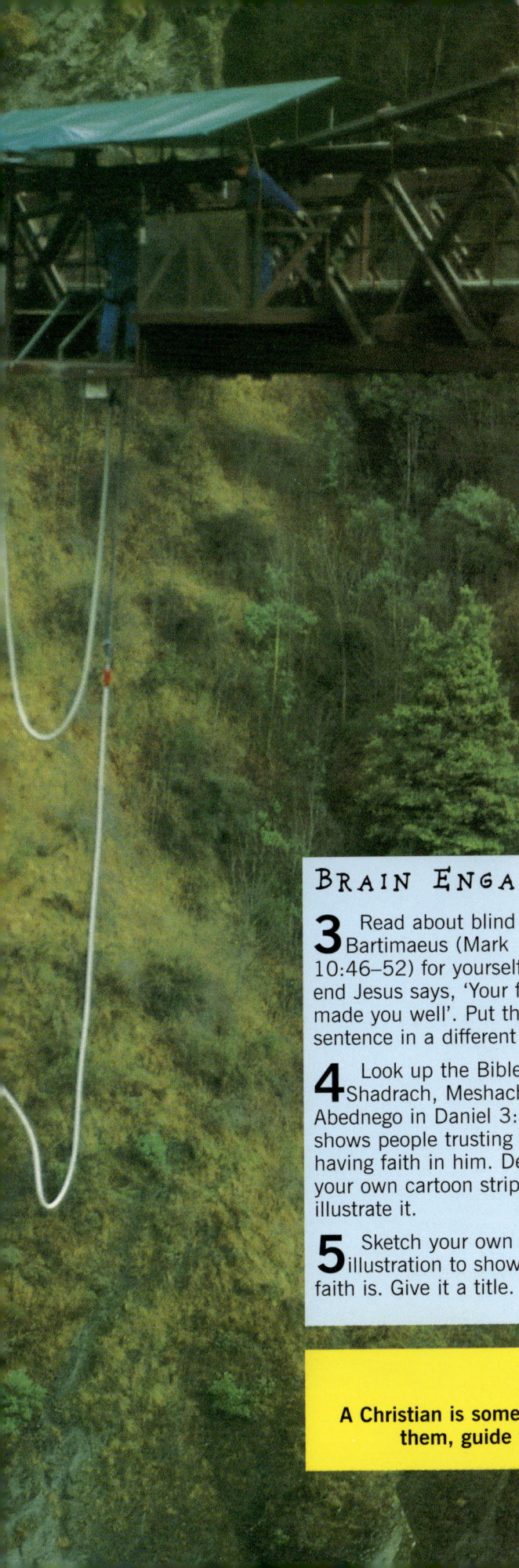

A Christian is someone who has faith in God. Christians are people who depend upon and trust in God day by day. When considering how they should act in any given situation they seek God's guidance, thereby showing they have faith in him.

Faith in God is like the rope connecting the climber with safety. It is a basic trust in God.

The Bible is full of stories of people who have shown faith in God. One example is the story of a blind man.

Blind Bartimaeus

As Jesus was leaving Jericho with his disciples and a large crowd, a blind beggar called Bartimaeus was sitting by the road. When he heard that it was Jesus of Nazareth, he began to shout for Jesus to take pity on him. Jesus stopped and asked that Bartimaeus come to him. The blind man threw off his cloak, jumped up, and came at once. When Jesus asked Bartimaeus what he wanted, he said, 'Teacher, I want to see again.'

Jesus replied, 'Go, your faith has made you well.'

At once he was able to see and he followed Jesus on the road.

Where there was no faith, healing was impossible and Jesus was powerless to help. Christians do not believe that faith is an easy thing; it requires courage and effort.

66 When things are going OK it is easier to trust God, but when things are not going well it's more difficult to have faith in him. Trusting in God is something I have to practise day by day. 99

Tim, 19

BRAIN ENGAGE

3 Read about blind Bartimaeus (Mark 10:46–52) for yourself. At the end Jesus says, 'Your faith has made you well'. Put that sentence in a different way.

4 Look up the Bible story of Shadrach, Meshach and Abednego in Daniel 3:8–30. It shows people trusting God—having faith in him. Design your own cartoon strip to illustrate it.

5 Sketch your own illustration to show what faith is. Give it a title.

SUMMARY
A Christian is someone who has faith in God—faith that God will help them, guide them and be with them through all dangers.

Religious Experience

Christians believe that God guides them in the choices they make. This unit explores what it means to say that God speaks to people today.

Some of the world's great scientists and artists have said that their best ideas have come to them in flashes of inspiration. For example, Pasteur's discovery of the cause of anthrax, Newton's realization of the force of gravity and Einstein's intuition which led to the theory of relativity came in moments of illumination— Newton's inspiration was triggered simply by an apple falling on his head.

The Bible is full of accounts of people who have been inspired by God. The word which is used to speak of this communication is 'revelation', in which God 'reveals' himself to people. For example, God spoke to Moses through nature (Exodus 3); Isaiah had a vision of God sitting upon a throne (Isaiah 6); and Paul heard a voice from God as he travelled on the road to Damascus (Acts 9). People continue to be inspired by God in real ways in their lives today.

What is happening? What sort of conversations are taking place in these pictures? What questions would you like to ask these people?

❝ When people talk of having a religious experience, it is not always something dramatic. Sometimes it can feel like the bits and pieces of a jigsaw coming together— events starting to make sense, being given an understanding of where I am going in life. ❞

Chris

❝ God doesn't talk to me in a dramatic way but I feel that God talks to me regularly—he puts ideas into my head and makes me think I should do something. If the thought keeps recurring I know I should do something about it. ❞

Matt

1 Have you ever had an experience like the scientists and artists mentioned in this unit—that you have been given a sudden illumination or answer on a problem—a flash of insight?

2a Have you ever had an experience which you would say is religious? What made the experience religious?

2b In the account of Isaiah's encounter with God, he felt as though he had come into the presence of something holy. What do you think it means to call something holy?

2c Have you ever felt that you have come into the presence of something which is holy?

3a Read through the accounts of people in the Bible who say they have encountered God. Make a list of ways in which these people have encountered God.

3b What questions would you like to ask any of these people?

3c In what ways do their encounters affect the rest of their life?

4a Christians encounter God when they pray. But what is prayer? Why do you think people pray?

4b C.S. Lewis is a well-known Christian who wrote the children's books known as the Narnia Chronicles. He said, 'I pray because I can't help myself. I pray because the need flows out of me all the time. It doesn't change God, it changes me.' What do you think he meant? Do you agree with him?

4c In what ways do you think prayer changes somebody? What do you think C.S. Lewis meant when he said that prayer doesn't change God?

'The force be with you'

Christians believe that God has given his living presence to people, the Holy Spirit. Christians believe that God's Holy Spirit works within them in a number of ways:

✗ to change people—to make them more like God

✗ to make them clean inside when they have done things wrong—this is called God's forgiveness

✗ to comfort people

✗ to give people wisdom and knowledge of what God requires of them.

66 God speaks through his word, the Bible. Sometimes I can read the Bible and know that God is saying something special to me. God's Holy Spirit helps me to understand his word. 99

John

66 At the centre of religion is a relationship and a conversation. My father thought the voice was outside of him, and I feel it inside me. But if you chat with God all your life, you do get to know him as you do a friend or a father. 99

Heirut

Paul the apostle said that you should be able to see the 'fruit of the Spirit' at work in a Christian's life:

The Spirit produces love, joy, peace, patience, kindness, goodness, faithfulness, humility and self-control.

Galatians 5:22–23

Christians know that it is a lifelong task to develop these qualities; it doesn't just happen overnight.

Making sense of life is like fitting a jigsaw together.

SUMMARY
Christians believe that God speaks to them and guides them in the choices they make in life.

❏ Is it easy to forgive?

❏ Look at the following story. If you were the family of Philip Lawrence could you forgive?

15TH DECEMBER 1995

Head stabbed at school gates

Philip Lawrence, head of St George's School in London, died from a single stab wound after rushing to help 13-year-old William Njoh who was being harassed by a group of youths outside the school gates.

The National Association of Head Teachers has reports of a record 69 cases of assaults or violent verbal abuse against its members this year.

Based on *Times Educational Supplement*, 15 December 1995

BRAIN ENGAGE

1 In pairs, discuss occasions when you have done something wrong and have either been forgiven or not been forgiven. What does it feel like for someone to hold a grudge against you? What does it feel like to be forgiven?

2 There is a saying 'To make mistakes is human but to forgive is divine'. Why do we sometimes find it difficult to forgive people?

3a Jesus taught a lot about forgiveness. Look up the following passages and make a list of the things which Jesus said: Matthew 5:38–39; Matthew 5:43–45; Matthew 18:21–35.

3b Jesus also taught that if someone has done something to you you must not wait for that person to come and ask your forgiveness, you must go out of your way to make peace with that person yourself (Matthew 5:23–24). What do you think?

4 Christians believe that they are called to forgive people. Use the quotes on this page to write a paragraph explaining what forgiveness means.

In Philip Lawrence's funeral service, his daughter said the following prayer:

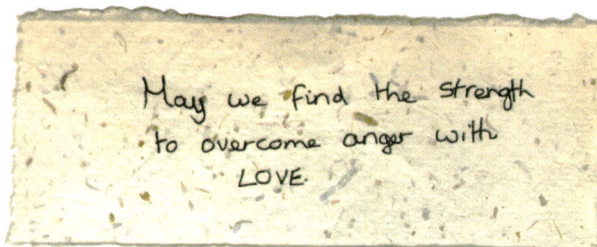

May we find the strength to overcome anger with LOVE.

One of the most difficult things which Jesus commanded his followers to do was to forgive— even those people who were their enemies. When Peter, one of Jesus' disciples, asked Jesus whether he should forgive a person as much as seven times, Jesus answered, 'Not seven but seventy times seven.' (Matthew 18:22) Jesus then told a story about a servant eager to be forgiven a debt by his master but unwilling to show mercy to a fellow-servant. (Matthew 18:23–35) This story was to highlight the need to forgive each other as God forgives us— unconditionally, however many times we have already been asked for forgiveness.

Help to forgive

It is never easy to forgive. However, anyone who has benefited from being forgiven may be moved to forgiving someone who has made a mistake like their own. Christians say that knowing God has forgiven them helps them be more forgiving to others.

❝ Me Dad went to prison and we have to keep remembering to love him. ❞

Jean, 7 (From *Lots of Love* by Nanette Newman, Collins)

A sandy beach is smoothed flat by the tide. Why do you think some people find this a useful image of forgiveness?

66 Although a person is forgiven they still have to live with the consequences of their actions. For example, if someone has been violent to another person, it is right that they receive punishment, in prison for example. We believe in a God of justice. But this does not mean that they cannot be forgiven and given a fresh start as well. The same with me: God has forgiven me for the things I have done wrong in the past but I have to live with the emotional scars of what I have done. I learn from them. 99

Sonia, 25

66 To forgive someone is not the natural thing to do. Some years ago my wife left me for someone else. I was so angry and felt rejected. The bitterness kept gnawing away at me until one night I could stand it no longer. Although I didn't want to forgive her I knew I had to if the anger was not going to destroy me. But I couldn't forgive. I prayed to God to take away the bitterness and to help me to forgive Ann. That night I slept peacefully for the first time in months. God's love helped me to forgive. 99

James, 34

66 Being forgiven is like being healed. 99

Craig, 16

66 In order to keep our forgiveness up to date we should be doing it every day. 99

Chuck

SUMMARY
Christians believe that God forgives them for what they do wrong and that they are called to pass on God's forgiveness to others. Christians believe that everyone deserves countless fresh chances.

11 Love is a Difficult Word

❏ Which of these people would you find it easy to love? Which would you find difficult to love? Say why.

❏ What qualities would a person need to love each of the people in the photographs?

Answer the above question by completing the sentence 'Love is…'

❏ What kind of people are difficult to love? How might love change them? What does real love consist of?

The idea of love stands at the centre of Christian moral teaching. Jesus summarized his teaching on right and wrong in his reply to a Jewish teacher who asked him which was the most important rule in life. He answered by saying, 'Love the Lord your God with all your heart, with all your soul, with all your mind, and with all your strength. The second most important commandment is this: "Love your neighbour as you love yourself." ' (Mark 12:29–31).

The Jewish teachers at the time of Jesus taught that people should follow God's lead: God is loving to all—he sends rain on the just and the unjust. So also, people should love all people. Where Jesus was different was that he extended this principle by saying that people should love even their enemies: 'You have heard that it was said, "Love your friends, hate your enemies." But now I tell you: love your enemies and pray for those who persecute you.' (Matthew 5:43–44)

One of Jesus' disciples wrote:

Dear friends, let us love one another, because love comes from God. Whoever does not love does not know God, for God is love. We love because God first loved us. If someone says he loves God, but hates his brother, he is a liar.

1 John 4:7–8, 19

24

1 What did Jesus teach about love? How did he differ from the other teachers of his day? Do you think his teaching is realistic? Explain your answer.

2 The principle of love is not an easy thing to carry out. It means wanting the best for others. What do you think is the most loving thing to do in each of the following situations?

♦ One of your closest friends is very unhappy. She feels that nobody likes her. But the main reason why people don't talk to her any longer is because she speaks behind people's backs. What is the most loving thing to do?

♦ You discover that one of your friends is taking drugs, but you don't think anyone else suspects. If your friend is found out, she/he will be in trouble. What is the most loving thing to do?

♦ Life at home has become really hard recently. Your mum seems to be always nagging you and blaming you for everything that goes wrong. The main reason she is in such a foul mood is because your dad left home a month ago for another woman. What is the most loving way of dealing with the situation?

3 Mini essay: Using quotes from the Bible explain the Christian concept of love. Is this teaching important for today's world?

Christians believe that the ability to love like this disciple comes from God. Totally unselfish love does not come naturally: people have to ask God to help them change. Christians want to love even though they find it difficult to do so and at times fail miserably.

What do you think love is? Here is a list from a letter to new Christians included in the Bible (1 Corinthians 13). Which of these qualities do you think is the most important when you love someone? Say why.

✔ Love is patient—it never gives up.

✔ Love is kind—it cares more for others than for self.

✔ Love isn't jealous.

✔ Love doesn't boast and isn't proud.

✔ Love is not rude.

✔ Love is not selfish—isn't always 'me first'.

✔ Love isn't irritable—it doesn't fly off the handle.

✔ Love does not count up the wrongs of others.

✔ Love is not happy with evil, but is happy with the truth.

✔ Love never gives up.

This little girl was hideously disfigured by illness. People with a special love and concern for victims like her have been able to change things. The picture on the right shows how she looks today.

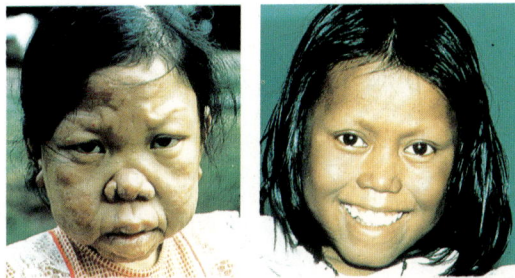

❏ **This girl had her appearance transformed because people loved her. How else do people change if they are loved rather than rejected?**

SUMMARY
Christians believe they must obey Jesus' command to love. It is an extravagant love: they are called to love all people as God does—enemies as well as friends.

Being Counted

❏ **Have you ever had to be a representative for your school or an organization or club to which you belong?**

❏ **What does it feel like to stand up in front of people and give a speech?**

An ambassador is an important official who lives in a foreign country and represents his or her own country's interests there. In the Bible, Christians are described as Christ's ambassadors: 'We have been sent to speak for Christ.' (2 Corinthians 5:20) Christians believe they are called to carry out Jesus' policies here on earth by loving others, forgiving others, serving others and by working for justice in the world.

Teresa of Avila (1515–1582) made the same point when she described Christians as Christ's hands and feet in today's world:

Christ has no body now on earth but yours,
no hands but yours, no feet but yours.
You are the eyes through which must look out
Christ's compassion on the world.
Yours are the feet with which he is to go about
doing good.
Yours are the hands with which he is to bless
others now.

Being an ambassador for Christ can be costly. In the early days of Christianity many Christians were persecuted and killed for what they believed. The amazing thing is that Christians are still dying for their faith in many parts of the world today.

❝ At no time in these 500 years have there been so many martyrs among the ministers of the Church as there are today. ❞

Erwin Krautler, of the Latin American Church, Brazil

Many Christians have had to show great courage in standing against injustice.

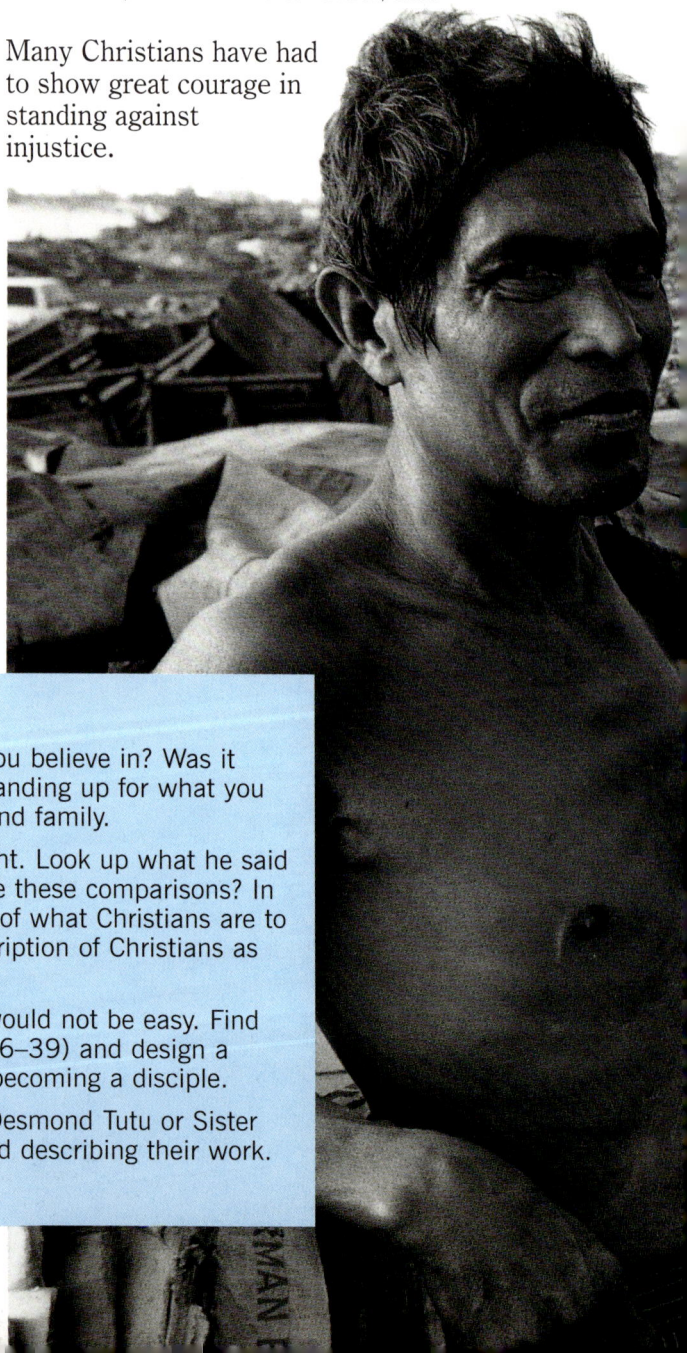

BRAIN ENGAGE

1 Have you ever had to stand up for something you believe in? Was it easy? In small groups discuss occasions when standing up for what you believe may make you unpopular with your friends and family.

2 Jesus compared Christians to being salt and light. Look up what he said in Matthew 5:13–16. Why do you think he made these comparisons? In what ways do you think these are good descriptions of what Christians are to be? How does this description fit in with Paul's description of Christians as 'ambassadors' for Christ?

3 Jesus warned his disciples that following him would not be easy. Find out what he said (Mark 8:34–35; Matthew 10:16–39) and design a WARNING poster for anyone who is thinking about becoming a disciple.

4 Use your library to find out more about either Desmond Tutu or Sister Emmanuelle. Design and write a magazine spread describing their work.

Desmond Tutu was the Archbishop of Cape Town, South Africa. He was a leading figure who spoke out against apartheid in order to bring equality between blacks and whites. 'When he encounters injustice God always takes sides… He is a God of surprises, uprooting the powerful and the unjust to establish his kingdom.' He is now the chairperson of the Truth and Reconciliation Commission which aims to find out the truth of the crimes which were committed against the black people and bring about national forgiveness and reconciliation, not revenge.

When she was over 60, Sister Emmanuelle went to share the life of the rubbish collectors in Cairo, Egypt, who live by collecting scraps from the rubbish which they sell in order to buy food. She then went on to raise money for schools and medical centres. Her courage in sharing God's love in a real way changed many lives.

The picture below shows a family living on a rubbish tip in Manila in the Philippines. Would you want to do voluntary work to help here?

SUMMARY
• • • • • • • • • • • • • •
Christians are Christ's ambassadors on earth. They are to carry out his policies. This can be a costly experience.

13 The Valley of Decision

We have seen that all of us look at the world through spectacles which are made up of our values and beliefs. In this first section of the book we have been looking at Christian beliefs and values—the spectacles through which Christians see the world.

This page summarizes two views of the world which Christians see as they look through their spectacles and try to make moral decisions.

Civil war

Sometimes a war is not between different countries but between different people within the same country. This is called a 'civil' war—it is between 'civilians' of the same country.

Christians sometimes use this image of a civil war to explain what is going on in the universe at large. The Bible tells a story that in the beginning 'war broke out in heaven. Michael and his angels fought against the dragon… The huge dragon was thrown out—that ancient serpent called the Devil, or Satan. He was thrown down to earth, and all his angels with him.' (Revelation 12:7–9)

Christians believe that there has been some sort of rebellion against God and it has been partly successful. The Devil and his angels have taken over, and to a great extent, are the rulers of this world.

Christians therefore believe that there is some kind of civil war going on and we are taking sides all our lives. In the decisions we make in life we either collaborate with the

BRAIN ENGAGE

1 What evidence is there in the world today to support the Christian belief that the Devil is the ruler of the world? Brainstorm your ideas as a class.

2 Draw a picture to show the meaning of Macarius' description of the human heart. (See top of page 29)

How could you compare the physical destruction in the photo with the destruction caused by evil in the world?

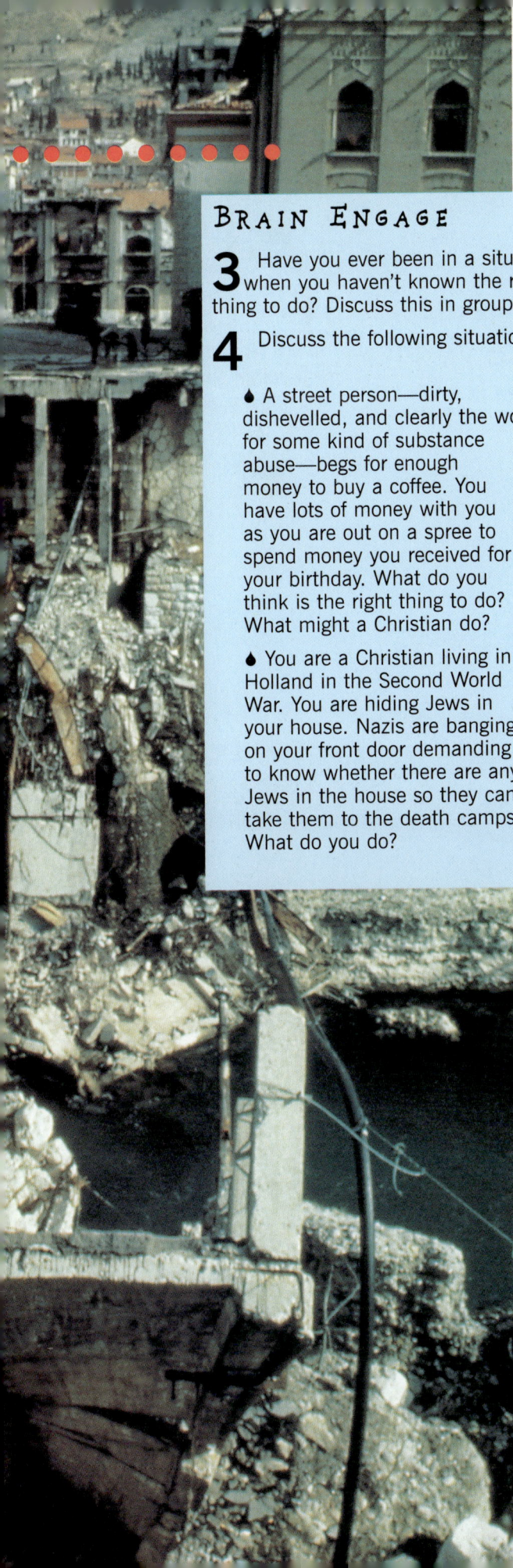

present ruler of this world—the Devil —or we accept God's final kingship in the world.

Within the heart are unfathomable depths. It is but a small vessel and yet dragons and lions are there, and gaping chasms. There likewise is God, there are the angels, there life and the Kingdom, there light and the Apostles, the heavenly cities and the treasures of grace: all things are there.

The Homilies of St Macarius

The search

Have you ever been in a place where you can only see a few inches in front of you? What does it feel like?

This image of searching for the way in the middle of the fog is a good picture of what life can sometimes feel like. Sometimes you want to do what is right in a situation but you are not at all clear what is right or wrong. Making moral decisions can feel like being caught in a thick fog where you can only see the next step in front of you and not the full consequences of any action you might take.

The Bible describes life on earth as a 'valley of decision' (Joel 3:14, New International Version)—the decisions people make are important because they take a person closer to God or push them further away from God.

BRAIN ENGAGE

3 Have you ever been in a situation when you haven't known the right thing to do? Discuss this in groups.

4 Discuss the following situations:

◆ A street person—dirty, dishevelled, and clearly the worse for some kind of substance abuse—begs for enough money to buy a coffee. You have lots of money with you as you are out on a spree to spend money you received for your birthday. What do you think is the right thing to do? What might a Christian do?

◆ You are a Christian living in Holland in the Second World War. You are hiding Jews in your house. Nazis are banging on your front door demanding to know whether there are any Jews in the house so they can take them to the death camps. What do you do?

SUMMARY

Christians believe that in the moral choices people make they are either cooperating with God or collaborating with the Devil.

The Miracle of Life

❏ **Look at the photograph of the baby at the bottom of the page. Why do you think the birth of a baby is sometimes called a miracle?**

❏ **What is it about newborn babies which makes them so special?**

If you look at the details of nature—the wings of a dragonfly, the veins of a leaf, the way the whole cycle of nature fits together—there is the same attention to detail as you see in the tiny fingers of a newborn baby, each of which has its own unique mark. No two people have the same set of fingerprints. From one strand of a person's hair, their unique genetic code can be determined. Many people believe that such detail points to a design in life.

❏ **Do you think life is an accident or does it have a meaning? Give reasons for your answer.**

BRAIN ENGAGE

1a Draw around one of your hands. In the space write 'I'M AMAZING'.

1b Write on each of the fingers something which is unique about you.

1c Now describe what life might be like if we were all the same.

2 Illustrate James Weldon Johnson's poem of creation (see opposite page), taking care to bring out the religious meanings in it. What do you think it means to say that people are created in the image of God? Consider the following qualities of God and how these are reflected in people—Creator God, loving God, just God, God who makes promises.

3a Look up Psalm 8:3–5. What does this psalm say about the value of human life?

3b What does it mean to say that life is sacred?

3c How do you think this belief affects how Christians treat life?

3d What might this say to them about such issues as abortion, suicide, euthanasia?

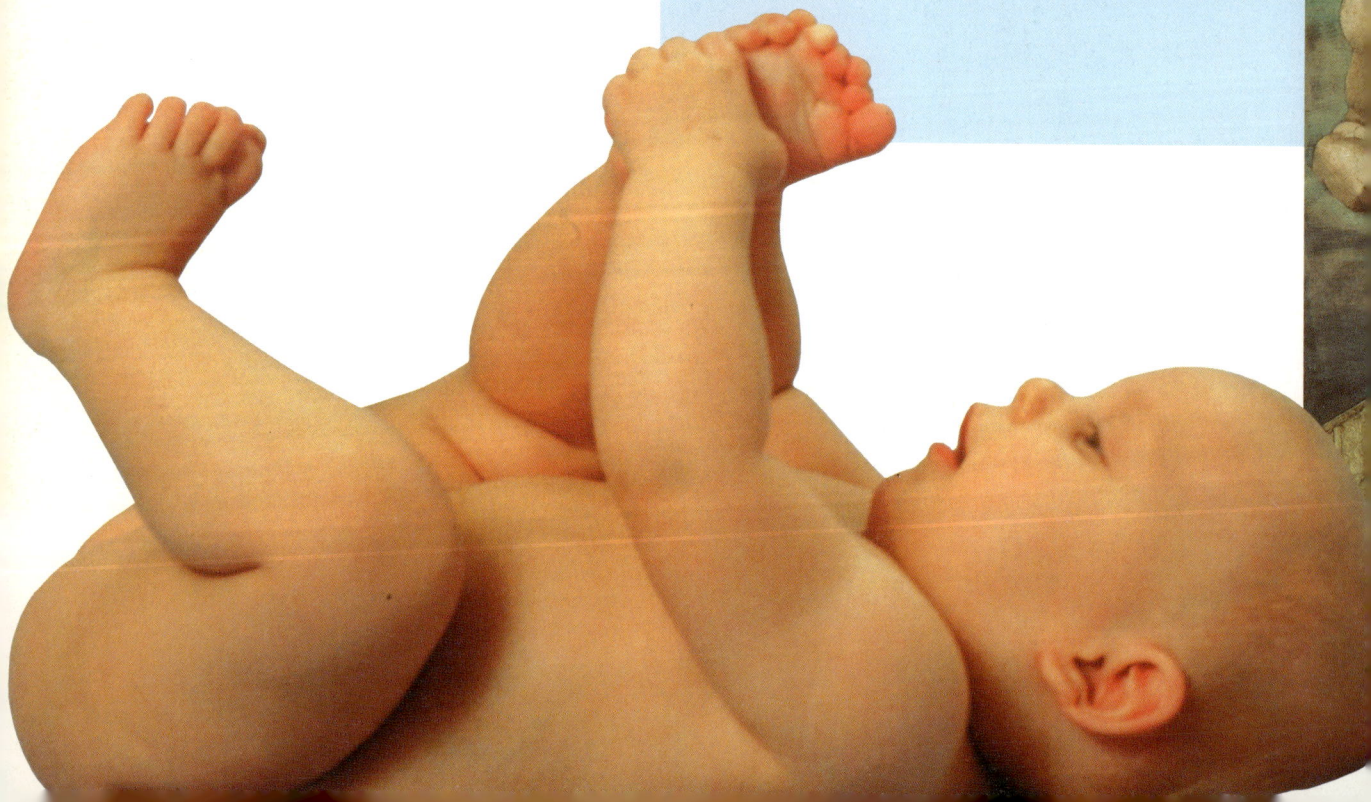

Christians believe that life is not just the result of an accident but is a miracle designed by a Creator God. In the following poem, James Weldon Johnson retells the biblical story of the creation of people.

❏ **As you read it what picture of the Creator God do you get?**

Then God sat down
On the side of a hill where he could think;
By a deep, wide river he sat down;
With his head in his hands,
God thought and thought,
Till he thought, I'll make me a man!

Up from the bed of the river
God scooped the clay;
And by the bank of the river
He kneeled him down;
And there the great God Almighty
Who lit the sun and fixed it in the sky,
Who flung the stars to the most far corner of the night,
Who rounded the earth in the middle of his hand;
This great God,
Like a mammy bending over her baby,
Kneeled down in the dust
Toiling over a lump of clay
Till he shaped it in his own image;
Then into it he blew the breath of life,
The man became a living soul.
Amen. Amen.

James Weldon Johnson, from 'The Creation'

Christians believe that each human life is a miracle made in the image of God. (Genesis 1:27, 9:6) They believe that life is sacred.

You made me and formed me with your hands.

Psalm 119:73

In units 14–28 we will be exploring issues which affect us personally—for example, issues to do with personal identity, our families, and our sexuality. We will end this section by considering the use of money and how we use our speech.

How does Michelangelo try to show in this painting that humanity was not created by accident?

SUMMARY
Christians believe that life is a miracle created and planned by God. Each person is unique, made in God's image and special to God.

Body Beautiful?

Is there such a thing as an ideal body? If so which of these photographs is nearest this ideal? Explain why.

❏ **Are looks important? Explain your answer. Do you choose your friends because of the way they look?**

Human bodies come in a whole range of shapes, sizes and colours. Many people do not think that their shape or size is ideal. This is what a number of young people thought about their bodies:

66 I wish I wasn't so fat—I just can't help putting on weight; it's not that I eat unhealthily. 99

Julia, 13

66 My face is full of spots; why can't I be like other people? 99

Richard, 14

📁 **BIBLE FILE**

✚ God looked at everything made in creation and was very pleased. (Genesis 1:31) If this is true, the human body is to be valued and cared for, whatever the shape.

✚ 'You do not belong to yourselves but to God.' (1 Corinthians 6:19) Our bodies are a gift from God; they are 'on loan'. People have a responsibility to look after them, and not to abuse them.

✚ 'Don't you know that your body is the temple of the Holy Spirit, who lives in you… so use your body for God's glory.' (1 Corinthians 6:19–20)

✚ The Bible teaches that people are not just to follow the fashions of the world—'Do not conform yourselves to the standards of this world.' (Romans 12:2)

✚ Christians believe people are more than their bodies. 'God does not see the same way people see. People look at the outside of a person, but the Lord looks at the heart.' (1 Samuel 16:7)

66 God made me the way I am and therefore I would not dream about changing myself, not even dyeing my hair. **99**

Janet, 15

66 I don't think looks are important; it's how you are on the inside that counts. **99**

Stephanie, 14

❏ **What do you feel about your body? Write your own speech bubble.**

Anita Roddick is founder of The Body Shop:

66 It's only in the last two centuries that we've defined beauty as the appearance. To my mind, it is a dimension of action... of courage. It's about compassion... The notion that beauty is only a physical combination of features is ludicrous. **99**

As quoted in *Third Way*, April 1996

Whose body is it anyway?

Do you think that you have a right to do what you want with your body? For example, what if you wanted to wear a nose-ring, do your parents have a right or duty to stop you?

Are these punks making a statement about themselves or do they just like the way they look?

Some people argue that parents have their children's best interests at heart when they govern what they do with their body (for example, making a child wear a brace for their teeth).

Use or Abuse of the Body?

In the last unit we considered the Christian belief that people should use their bodies in responsible ways because they are 'on loan' from God. But what does it mean to use our bodies in irresponsible ways?

Sometimes a substance can be both acceptable and unacceptable depending upon the culture in which a person is living. For example, smoking tobacco is legal and in many places socially respectable. Does this mean that people are acting responsibly when they smoke?

❏ **The 'slimmer's disease' anorexia nervosa is estimated to affect one female in every hundred between the ages of 12 and 25. Why do some people slim to the extent of making themselves ill?**

> 66 **It doesn't matter how many times people tell you you're slim, or that you don't need to diet. What you see in the mirror is something completely different.** 99
>
> Sophie, 14

❏ **What do you make of Sophie's comment?**

❏ **Is it OK to feed the body _constantly_ with junk food?**

Some substances can be both good for the body and bad for the body. Some drugs are used as medicines to

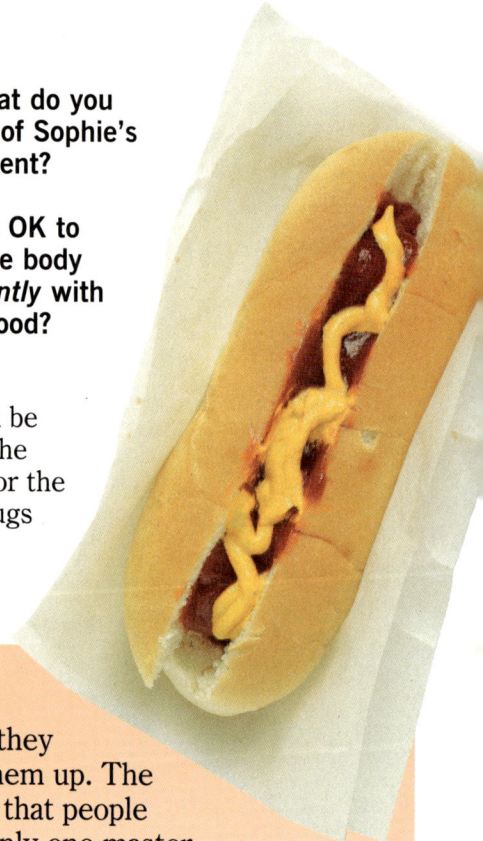

BIBLE FILE

The Bible says certain things about the use and abuse of the body. What it says about drink can also be applied to other drugs.

✚ Some people say that they can do what they want with their body. To this Paul replies in the Bible: 'Someone will say, "I am allowed to do anything." Yes; but not everything is good for you. I could say that I am allowed to do anything, but I am not going to let anything make me its slave.' (1 Corinthians 6:12)

✚ Paul tells people to be careful how they live. 'Don't live like ignorant people, but like wise people… Do not get drunk with wine, which will only ruin you.' (Ephesians 5:15, 18)

✚ Both drugs and food can become the most important thing in a person's life: they cannot give them up. The Bible teaches that people should have only one master, namely God.

✚ Christians believe that life is the most precious gift which God gives a person. When God created the world, he saw that it was good. If people take something which can harm them, they are destroying the good creation of God.

✚ For a Christian, the body is where God's Spirit lives and should therefore be treated with respect. (1 Corinthians 6:12–20)

✚ Christians are called to care for people who are weaker than them and not to put temptation in other people's way. (1 Corinthians 8:9)

help people. But even medicines, like paracetamol, can be very dangerous in a mild overdose. Therefore people need to take care to keep their bodies safe.

Tens of thousands of teenagers are believed to take Ecstasy tablets or Speed (amphetamine) every week when they attend clubs and dances. Ecstasy is known as a recreational drug, the 'happy pill' for the mood-altering effects it has on people. However, scientists are discovering the growing dangers of taking Es: the drug destroys nerve terminals in the brain; in periods between taking the drug, people can behave erratically— it can cause mood swings, panic attacks and loss of appetite. The tablets may cause brain damage and some young people have died from taking them.

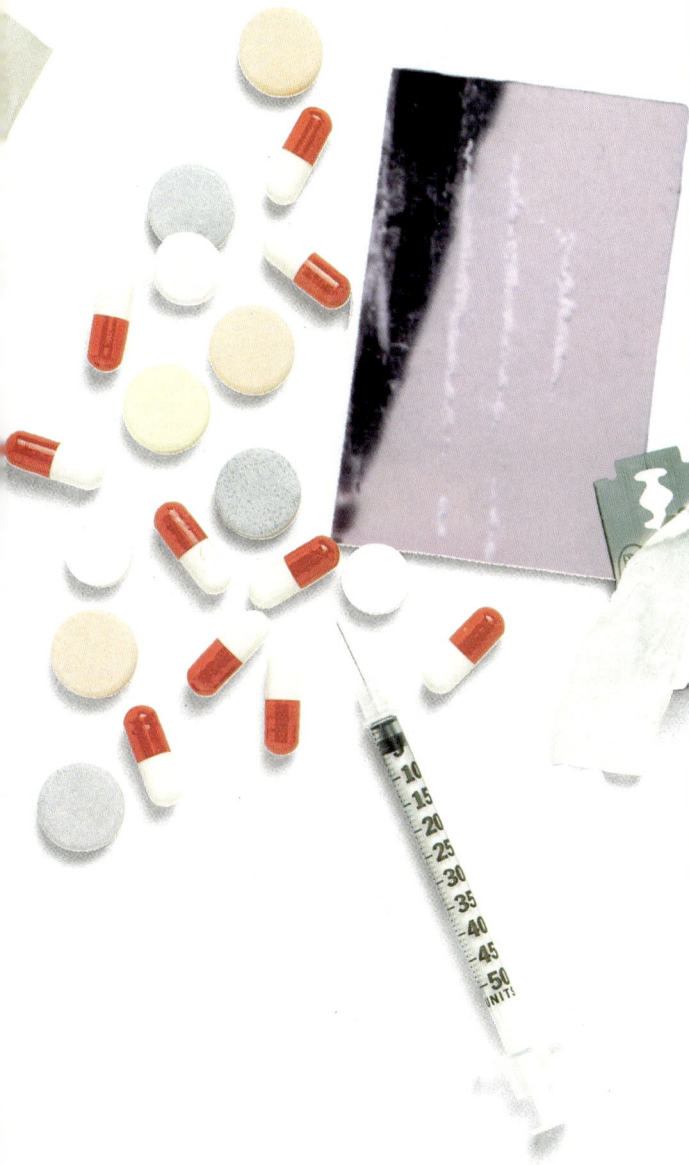

BRAIN ENGAGE

1a What is an 'addiction'?

1b Make a list of things people become addicted to.

1c What do you think Paul meant when he said in 1 Corinthians, 'I am not going to let anything make me its slave'? (1 Corinthians 6:12)

1d Make two columns in your book. In the left-hand column, write down the characteristics of a slave. In the right-hand column, apply these characteristics to smoking.

1e Look up what Paul says about a battle going on inside him in Romans 7:14–20. How is addiction to a drug like this battle?

2a Look at advertisements for cigarettes and alcoholic drinks. What message are these advertisers communicating about using these drugs?

2b Professor Sir Richard Doll, the first scientist to discover the dangers of tobacco in 1950, attacks the Government for refusing to ban tobacco advertising: 'I think it is immoral. Here is something that kills one sixth of the population and the Government allows advertisers to encourage people to do it.' Why do you think the Government allows advertising?

3a Imagine you are going to be put in charge of all meals in your household. Write a food policy statement explaining the principles guiding your choice of foods.

3b Use the Bible File to write a Christian charter for the body.

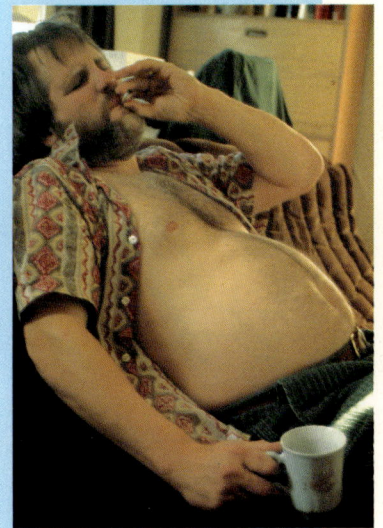

SUMMARY
Christians believe that when people abuse their bodies, they not only do themselves damage but are destroying what God created to be good.

37

Happy Families

Families come in all shapes and sizes. But they are usually thought of as a unit where there is a couple or perhaps where there are two or more generations committed to each other and caring for each other.

❏ **Share your idea of a family in small groups. How do your ideas differ from each other?**

📁 BIBLE FILE

Study the following biblical views. Talk about each in turn and feed back your responses to the rest of the class.

✚ 'Children are a gift from the Lord.' (Psalm 127:3) Jesus stressed the importance of caring for children. (Matthew 18:5–6)

✚ One of the Ten Commandments is 'Respect your father and your mother.' (Exodus 20:12; see also Proverbs 13:1)

✚ Paul wrote, 'Children, it is your Christian duty to obey your parents, for this is the right thing to do… Parents, do not treat your children in such a way as to make them angry. Instead, bring them up with Christian discipline and instruction.' (Ephesians 6:1–4)

✚ The way parents bring up their children should reflect how God deals with people. (Deuteronomy 8:5)

The Bible talks of the family as being a husband and wife who leave their parents to form a unit in which children are raised. However, the Bible does not present a glossy picture of the family. It recognizes that there are struggles within all families. Jesus told the parable of the lost son (Luke 15:11–32) illustrating the tension between children and parents. Read the story and make a list of the lessons which both parents and children could learn from it.

A man had two sons. One day the younger son came to him asking for his share of his inheritance so that he could have a good time and not have to wait until his father died. Because he loved his son, the father agreed and gave him his share of the money. That very day, the son left home with a big smile on his face, without thinking about what he was leaving behind—he was greedy for the life which lay ahead of him.

The son travelled to a far-off country. He drank. He gambled. He used his money on girls, until finally all the money had gone. He dared not return home so he started to look for a job. But the only job he could find was on a pig farm. As he slogged away at his job he thought that even his father's servants had a better life.

He decided to return home and ask for a job on his father's farm.

The father had spent every day waiting, hoping for his son to return. As soon as he saw him coming, he ran out to greet him and welcomed him with a great party: he embraced his son even though he stank like a pig, had damaged his family's reputation and wasted his fortune.

This is a strange story but Christians believe it was told to show how God, the perfect parent, remains committed to his children even though they turn away and reject all that he has taught them. Instead of judging and rejecting his son, the father in the story embraces him in love and forgives him, recognizing that the son is truly sorry for what he has done.

❏ **Do you think the father was right to give his son so much freedom?**

❏ **How can children offer this same quality of love to their parents?**

BRAIN ENGAGE

1 The Bible provides a number of descriptions of God as the ideal parent. Read each one and then make up a collage using the different images. What do these descriptions tell you about the biblical ideal of the family?

◆ God gives good things as a father should. (Matthew 7:7–11)

◆ God is compared to a mother hen who protects her chicks. (Luke 13:34)

◆ God is likened to a mother who comforts her child. (Isaiah 66:13)

◆ God is likened to a loving father who welcomes home the son who has run away. (Luke 15:31–32)

2a Think of a person who reflects some of God's attitudes towards people (e.g. shows caring, unconditional love and forgiveness; disciplines in a just way). Describe the person to a partner.

2b According to the Bible, parents should discipline their children. How does discipline differ from punishment?

3 If there was one thing which you could change in your family, what would it be?

4 Use the Bible File to describe two duties of children and three duties of parents.

5a Design a list of guidelines for creating a happy family.

5b You learn a lot at school but you are not taught how to be a parent. Why not?

5c What things do you think would have to be taught on such a course?

SUMMARY
• • • • • • • • • • •
Christians believe that God's unconditional love is a model for how people should treat one another.

Unhappy Families

In all families people disagree with each other. However, some families are more unhappy than they are happy. On this page we shall be looking at two causes of unhappiness for children in these families: divorce and abuse.

Divorce

66 I wish Mum and Dad still loved each other. 99

66 I feel as if an earthquake is happening. Once, my life was on solid ground. Now it's splitting and I'm having to choose which part to scramble to... but it's all crumbling. 99

Divorce is often a painful and messy process for all involved. How are children to cope with it?

Teenagers give advice about how to cope with divorce:

66 The most helpful thing someone said to me when my parents were splitting up was, 'It's not your fault'. As a child it is easy to think all the rows are because of you, but they're not. It might be your problem but it's not your fault. 99

Sonia

66 It's important to speak to your parents—get both of them to explain what is happening and why. Don't bottle up your own feelings—if you can tell your parents how you are feeling inside it should help you to cope. 99

Rachel

66 It's important to find an adult you can talk to and share your feelings with. 99

Ian

66 It's all right to be angry—it's natural. 99

John

The Bible contains many examples of parents who fail; for example Hosea's wife was constantly unfaithful to him but God urged Hosea to keep taking her back. Christians believe that Hosea's love for his wife is a little picture of God's love for us all. God never fails. Jesus spoke out against sin whilst at the same time behaving with compassion towards people who were hurting because of what they had done. How do you think this should influence a Christian in their reaction to a family which is coming apart due to divorce?

Abuse within the family

Parents have a duty to care, love and protect their own children. However, some children are not protected; instead they are abused. Abuse can take many forms—emotional, mental and physical. Physical abuse includes sexual abuse.

66 I just dread being left at home with my Dad. He tells me my Mum's no good in bed

but I can make it up to him. I hate everything he does and I hate my Mum for going out. 99

Samantha

66 My Mum's absolutely over the top about me and schoolwork. She's always nagging me to have top grades. I suppose that's what lots of kids would say. But when she said she'd commit suicide if I failed my exams, I thought I was going to crack up. 99

Mike

Childline: telephone 0800-1111

BRAIN ENGAGE

3 Vicki's mum's boyfriend has been abusing Vicki for six months. She is afraid that her mum won't believe her if she tells her and that if she does believe her, she will lose the man she loves.

3a If you were Vicki, whom would you tell (teacher, parent, church minister, another adult, a friend)?

3b Draft a letter asking for advice from Vicki to an agony aunt.

Childline is an organization which was set up to be a listening ear and give practical advice to children who feel they have nowhere else to turn. Alison turned to Childline because she felt that she could not talk to her parents or another adult: 'I was frightened I wouldn't be believed and scared that if I told Mum about what was happening I would be rejected and told off.'

Christians believe that God is on the side of all people who are abused.

BIBLE FILE

✚ Parents have a duty to care for their children and not to do anything which will make them angry [this includes abusing their children]. (Ephesians 6:4)

✚ Jesus understands what it feels like to be hurt and abused. He was vulnerable; on the cross his body was taken advantage of and broken.

✚ Jesus came to heal—to heal broken relationships; to offer healing to broken people. (Luke 4:18–19)

Christians are to be Christ-like friends to people in need. This is illustrated in the following story:

There was a young poet whose friend had lied to him and stolen his girlfriend, eventually marrying her. The poet fled because of his misery and became employed in a foreign court. Noticing the poet's sadness, the king felt full of sorrow himself. At first he offered the poet money, land and even a pretty girl but nothing would cheer him up. When the king asked the poet what he could do the poet replied, 'Come and sit with me and listen to my sorrow.' So every day the king did just that.

This story reflects the Christian belief that God is compassionate towards those who are hurting, and that we must try and follow God's example.

SUMMARY
• • • • • • • • • •
People in families fail each other. But Christians believe that God never fails, and with God's love they can change and be healed.

● ●

In this unit we explore some ideas about friendship. What does it mean to be a friend? During teenage years our friends become more and more important to us. This sometimes brings us into conflict with parents because they do not always like our choice of friends.

❏ **Do your parents like your choice of friends?**

❏ **What comments do they make about your friends?**

People learn to act differently depending on who they are with. Sometimes we feel under pressure to act in certain ways when we are with our friends. This is called 'peer pressure'.

Why do some people think they should never unfasten a friendship bracelet after they have agreed to wear it?

Tough situations

Sometimes people feel a conflict between showing loyalty to their friends and being honest. Consider the following situations. You may like to role-play them.

SITUATION 1

It's Thursday afternoon and you have just finished PE. As you are changing in the bathrooms, two of your friends start messing around. Accidentally, the bathroom door handle gets broken and the shower curtain is pulled off the wall. The next day at school all of you are questioned. What do you do? Do you say you were there? Do you tell the teacher that you know anything? Do you tell the teacher everything?

📁 BIBLE FILE

The Bible describes a number of characteristics of a good friend:

✛ 'Friends always show their love.' (Proverbs 17:17)

✛ A friend always has your best interests at heart, even when he hurts you. (Proverbs 27:6)

✛ When you do something wrong, a friend is someone who will point it out to you gently. (Galatians 6:1)

✛ A friend is willing to sacrifice things for you, even, if necessary, his life. (John 15:13)

✛ Jesus challenges people to 'love each other as I have loved you', that is self-sacrificially. (John 15:12) Jesus showed by his example that friends love people for who they are, not because they are rich or important. Jesus became friends with the outcasts of society—those that other people didn't love. (Matthew 11:19)

1a What makes a good friend? Here are a list of qualities you may look for in a friend:

- A good listener
- Someone you can have a laugh with
- Someone you can tell your secrets to
- Someone who lets you be yourself
- Loyalty
- Someone who doesn't gossip about you
- Someone who makes you laugh when you are hurting
- Someone who is always there for you
- Someone who stands by you in difficult times

Which do you think is the most important quality? Which other qualities do you look for in a good friend?

1b Could a person be cruel or untrustworthy or weak and still be your friend?

1c What makes a bad friend?

1d What breaks a friendship? What mends it?

1e How important is it to give and take in a friendship?

2 Name two ways in which you would act differently with your friends than you would with your parents.

3 Should friends always be loyal to each other? Describe a situation where (a) they should be and (b) they shouldn't be.

SITUATION 2

Your close friend asks you to tell her mother that she is staying at your house for a sleep-over when she is actually going to an all-night party. What do you do? How would you feel if the situation was the other way around and your friend didn't support you when you told your own mother a lie?

SITUATION 3

Your closest friend has betrayed your secrets to other people. What do you do?

SITUATION 4

You discover that a good friend of yours is taking drugs. What do you do, if anything? Do you tell somebody at school, at home, the police?

❏ **Now apply the biblical teaching on friendship to each situation. Does this make you act in different ways? Explain your answers.**

SUMMARY
• • • • • • • • • •
Friendship should always bring the best out in you—qualities of sacrifice, love, support and gentleness. At times, friendship with someone can require you to make difficult decisions.

15-year-old boy charged with killing another teenager in dispute over stolen bicycle

Bullies drove teenager to suicide

We are all capable of being violent, especially when we lose our temper. But newspaper headlines like these suggest that some teenage violence is out of all proportion to the cause.

In America, murder at school is now so commonplace that such incidents are often only reported in local newpapers.

16-year-old boy shoots unknown woman. Known as 'Little Rambo' to his schoolmates he told police that he 'just wanted to get away and kill somebody'.

❏ What feelings do you think instigated these crimes?

❏ Do you ever feel your anger is out of control?

📁 BIBLE FILE

✛ 'You shall not kill.' (Exodus 20:13)

✛ In the Bible, God's ideal is shown as peace and reconciliation. Jesus is called the Prince of Peace. (Isaiah 9:6)

✛ Jesus preached a message of non-violence. He told his disciples, 'You have heard that it was said, "An eye for an eye, and a tooth for a tooth." But now I tell you: do not take revenge on someone who wrongs you. If anyone slaps you on the right cheek, let him slap your left cheek too... love your enemies.' (Matthew 5:38–39, 44)

✛ Jesus backed up his message of non-violence by the way he acted. For example, when he was being arrested, he stopped Peter using his sword to defend him. Jesus chose to suffer an unjust death and not resist.

✛ 'Remember this... Everyone must be quick to listen, but slow to speak and slow to become angry.' (James 1:19)

✛ The Bible teaches that you should not pay back wrong with wrong—'Do not pay back evil with evil or cursing with cursing.' (1 Peter 3:9)

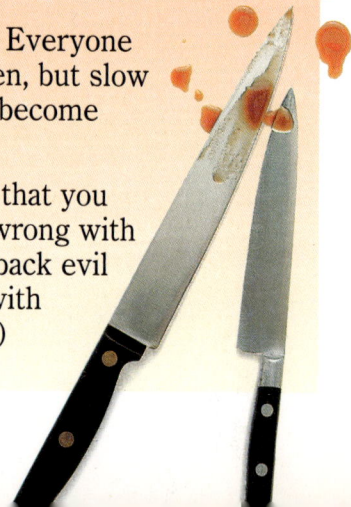

Brain Engage

1 When a group of teenagers were asked why they thought people were violent, they came up with a number of suggestions. Which do you agree with most and which do you agree with least?

66 Sometimes you have to use violence in self-defence. It's the only way that some people respect you and take you seriously. 99

Abe, 13

66 I think that part of the reason for the increase of violence is because there is so much violence on TV—especially if children see their heroes killing a lot of people and not feeling anything about it, like Rambo. 99

Jesse, 14

66 I think a lot of people are violent because they think life isn't fair to them, or they have troubles at home so they let their anger and unhappiness out on others. 99

Rebekka, 14

66 I think violence is an act of the Devil inside us. 99

Nicole, 14

66 When we get upset it is natural for us to want to lash out irrationally, but if we come from a stable background, we have been taught to control this anger. If you haven't been brought up to use self-discipline and control, it is easier to use violence. 99

Erika, 14

2a Carry out a TV Watch. Watch a selection of television programmes and make a note of all forms of violence that you see.

2b Do you think there should be less violence on television?

2c Do you think that acts of violence on television encourage youngsters to be violent?

3a Do you think that violence is ever justifiable? Try to think of an occasion when you think that the use of violence was the best option.

3b Do you think it is ever justifiable to kill another human being?

4 Do you think the teaching of the Bible on anger and violence is realistic? Explain your answer.

Summary
Jesus taught and practised a message of non-violence. God's ideal is peace and reconciliation.

According to the Bible, God created both man and woman as sexual beings. Sexuality is a part of each person's character. Whenever we relate to another person we do so as sexual beings. Sometimes this will be obvious (in a romantic relationship), but at other times we will hardly be aware of it. There is a wide range of ways in which we use our sexuality. Some people emphasize their sexuality in the way they dress and act. Others suppress their sexuality.

Which people in the photographs are showing their sexuality by the clothes they are wearing?

BIBLE FILE

✚ Men and women are to depend on each other. (1 Corinthians 11:11–12)

✚ Bodies are given by God and must be used responsibly in accordance with God's laws. We are to be stewards of our bodies. Sexual relationships with other people affect a person's relationship to God. (1 Corinthians 6:15–20)

✚ Thoughts are important as well as actions. 1 Corinthians 10:13 and 6:12 teaches that people should have the strength to dominate impure thoughts. What do you think counts as impure thoughts?

✚ All people are made in the image of God (Genesis 1:27–28), therefore they should not be treated in ways which dehumanize and exploit them.

BRAIN ENGAGE

1 Some magazines are devoted to providing pictures of naked or almost naked women, and many newspapers have such a picture on 'page 3'. Here are three opinions about using the human body in this way. Which do you most agree with? Say why.

66 **Offensive pictures of naked and semi-naked women in national newspapers should be banned. These pictures distort relationships between men and women.** 99

Clare Short, MP

66 **I don't think I'm being exploited at all. I believe in letting people do whatever they want to do.** 99

Rachel Garley, 21, Page 3 Model

66 **Why is it OK for women to have pin-ups of chests of men, with nipples showing, and not for men to have pictures of women?** 99

Mike

❏ **How might someone overplay their sexuality when choosing clothes? Why might they do this?**

We are not just sexual beings. It is important to get the balance right between our sexuality and other parts of our personality—our emotions, our thoughts, and our relationship with God. Christians believe that what people do with their bodies also affects their relationship with God. They therefore believe that a person's sexuality must not be misused.

Homosexuality

The word 'homosexual' refers to any man or woman who has a persistent sexual preference for members of the same sex. Female homosexuals are often called 'lesbians'. However, many people experience strong feelings towards people of the same sex when they are growing up. This does not necessarily mean that that person is a homosexual.

BIBLE FILE

✚ The Bible makes it clear that God created man and woman to become 'one flesh' within marriage. It says that people should not practise homosexual acts. (1 Corinthians 6:9–10; Leviticus 18:22, 20:13)

✚ Although homosexual relationships can be loving and faithful, they fall outside God's plan for people. This does not mean that God does not love homosexuals—God loves each individual as unique and wants each one— heterosexual and homosexual—to become the complete person they are meant to be through their relationship with God.

✚ Read Titus 3:2–3. What advice does this passage give? How might it help a Christian to know how to treat people who live in ways not recommended in the Bible?

BRAIN ENGAGE

2 Why do you think that the age of consent for heterosexuals is 16, but for homosexuals it is 18?

When a group of teenagers were asked what they thought about homosexuality, they expressed a wide range of views:

❝ **People have a right to choose how they express their sexuality.** ❞

Ruth

❝ **It's not their fault.** ❞

Charlotte

❝ **It's OK to be, but not to do.** ❞

John

❝ **God said, 'Adam and Eve' NOT 'Adam and Steve.'** ❞

Lauri

❝ **The only reason some people think it is wrong is because homosexuals are a minority and they are therefore an easy target to attack.** ❞

Nick

❏ **Discuss each of these views. Write your own opinion.**

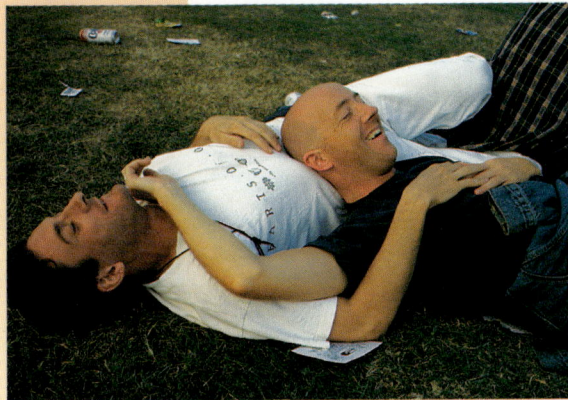

What reactions do you have to this photograph?

SUMMARY
• • • • • • • • • • • •
God made people sexual beings. People express their sexuality in a variety of ways. Christians believe their sexuality should be expressed in ways that are compatible with God's wishes.

GoingO u t

During adolescence, many people start forming close friendships with people outside their family group. Sometimes these develop into boyfriend and girlfriend relationships.

Issue 1: Why 'go out'?

When a group of teenagers were asked what they looked for in such relationships, they gave a variety of replies:

> 66 Someone who has the same values and beliefs and makes me feel worthwhile. 99

Abie, 15

> 66 To find someone who I can marry. 99

Jane, 17

> 66 Someone who is good-looking and with whom I can learn about sex. 99

James, 16

> 66 Someone who makes me feel I am liked and accepted. 99

David, 16

> 66 If I didn't have a boyfriend I would be the odd one out. 99

Sue, 16

❏ Which reason do you agree with (a) most (b) least? Give your reasons. Write your own reason for going out with someone.

Issue 2: How far can we go?

❏ Is kissing important in a relationship? In what ways can a kiss mean different things to different people? What might the two people in the photograph be feeling and thinking?

❏ How far should these two people go in being physical? On what criteria are you basing your decisions?

❏ What responsibility do you think these people have to each other?

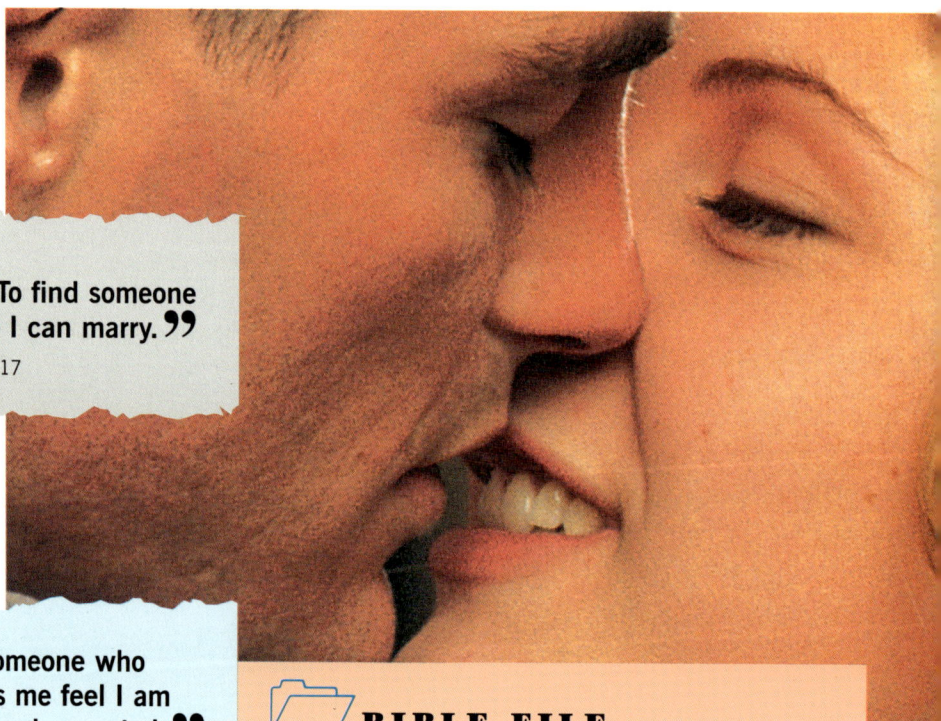

BIBLE FILE

Although the Bible does not specifically teach about boyfriend and girlfriend relationships—because in society then it wasn't an option—it gives guidelines which can apply to relationships generally.

✚ It teaches that the most important relationship a person can have is with Jesus. Another person should never take this place.

✚ It teaches that we should love our neighbour (i.e. each other) as we love ourselves. (Matthew 19:19) Christians need to ask themselves, 'Is what I am doing truly loving?'

BRAIN ENGAGE

1a Which of the following qualities do you think it is important to have in a boy/girlfriend? Rank them in order of importance giving '1' to the most important quality and '16' to the least important.

- good looks
- humility
- patience
- kindness
- intelligence
- loyalty
- similar religious beliefs to yourself
- hard-working

- forgiving
- honesty
- generosity
- athletic
- wealth
- wit
- talented
- popularity

1b If you were to add two more qualities what would they be? Say why.

2 Choose a magazine aimed at teenagers. How much of it is concerned with boy/girlfriend relationships? What sort of issues are they dealing with? Do you think that the magazine encourages these relationships? What does it say about how people should act in these relationships? Is the message these magazines give balanced?

3a In pairs, discuss each of the following comments about boy/girlfriend relationships saying whether you agree or disagree with it. Give your reasons.

66 **You must always be honest with your boy/girlfriend even when things aren't going well.** 99

66 **You mustn't try and possess the other person. You must give them freedom to be their own person. You shouldn't stop them seeing other friends.** 99

66 **You should discuss the relationship with your parents and seek their advice.** 99

3b Look through the biblical teaching on relationships. Choose two of the above comments and discuss them in the light of this teaching.

One of the commonest questions which boyfriends and girlfriends ask is 'How far can we go?' Usually, the question relates to the physical side of the relationship. However, when people start going out, they share information with each other—they become emotionally intimate, sharing secrets, hopes and fears. How far should they allow the emotional link to go? Not surprisingly, the closer people become, the harder it is if the relationship splits.

66 **The Bible doesn't say you can't kiss etc. The Bible is not a book of rules. Instead, what is important is to remain sexually pure for God. This involves a lot more than just remaining a virgin—it is not just a matter of not doing something. Instead it is a whole lifestyle. Instead of seeing how much you can 'get away with' in a relationship, ask yourself, 'What should a follower of Jesus do?' Sexual purity is like a valuable treasure—to be protected and kept safe.** 99

Richard, 17

Christians believe that relationships do not exist for selfish reasons. People should be willing to give as well as get in a relationship. They exist to help each other grow, emotionally and spiritually, into the person God wants them to become. For a Christian an important question is 'Is this relationship helping or hindering my growth?'

SUMMARY
Christians believe that in all human friendships they should help people in their relationship with God.

49

I am 16 and have been going out with my boyfriend for 10 months. He's 18. We love each other and have a great time together. But in the last few weeks he has been wanting us to have sex. I do love him, but I'm not sure I want to have sex with him. I'm still a virgin. I am frightened of losing him if I don't. I don't know what to do.

Confused Helen

❏ **What should Helen do?**

❏ **What are the issues involved in this letter?**

THE PLEDGE

'Believing that true love waits, I make a commitment to God, myself, and my family, those I date, my future mate, and my future children, to be sexually pure until the day I enter a covenant marriage relationship.'

True love waits

In America, many teenagers are joining a campaign which states that the best sex is no sex at all until marriage. The national movement started in 1992 when two 16-year-old girls told their minister, Reverend Richard Ross, that they felt stupid being the only virgins at their school. He started the 'True Love Waits' campaign to show that they were not alone. The 'True Love Waits' campaign encourages teenagers to make a

BIBLE FILE

✠ *Don't misuse your body.* 'Your body is the temple of the Holy Spirit who lives in you.' (1 Corinthians 6:19)

✠ *Sex is best celebrated within a marriage relationship.* The Bible speaks out against sex outside marriage.
(1 Corinthians 6:13, 18; Colossians 3:5; 1 Thessalonians 4:3)

✠ *If you make mistakes and regret it you can start again.* People often make mistakes in issues concerning sex and feel in need of a new start. Jesus taught that people should be given second chances. The Bible contains the moving account of when a woman who had been caught in adultery was brought to Jesus—he forgave her and challenged her to give up her immoral life and start afresh. (John 8:1–11)

promise (a pledge) not to have sex until they are married. The campaign is expanding to 150 countries worldwide, including Britain.

The campaign is not only about keeping pure and avoiding the risks of AIDS, for example. It is also a way for people to reclaim their virginity. For example, Kelly Hurly is 26 and has slept with more men than she can remember. By taking the pledge she is hoping to right the wrongs of the past:

66 The next time I sleep with someone, it'll mean something and I'll be married. 99

Kelly, 26

66 There are two reasons I signed the pledge—one is that God led me to do it, and the other is that there are so many problems if you do have sex before marriage. 99

Laura, 14

❏ What problems do you think Laura may be thinking of?

These are one person's guidelines to a teenage girl:

Only have sex because you want to.

✘ Not because he says he loves you.

✘ Not because your friends will think you're boring if you don't.

✘ Not because it's legal.

✘ Not because your best friend says it's really great.

✘ Not because you think he'll dump you if you don't.

What do you think of them? What would be your guidelines?

BRAIN ENGAGE

1a Jill Knight, MP, made this observation:

66 Look at some of the teenage magazines read by 11 to 13-year-olds. The whole impetus and pressure in them is to suggest that really the only fun thing to do is to have sex... 99

Do you agree with this statement? In what other ways are teenagers under pressure to have sex before marriage? How do pop songs present the issue of sex before marriage—are they encouraging it?

1b Choose one of the following opinions to discuss in small groups. Feedback your opinions on it to the rest of the class:

66 You look at teenage magazines and there's so much input about sex, and it's all so glamorous. And then you turn to the problem pages and you see the reality that desperate people are pregnant, people are so frightened, and the damage that sex can do. 99

Annie, 19

66 I think the emotional consequences of teenage sex is this feeling that you've given yourself but you haven't got anything back and it can make a very empty feeling—that you've done something that is supposed to be 'making love' and hardly any of the girls who write to me refer to it as 'making love'—which is what sex is in a very stable relationship. They mistake sex as a passage to adulthood and a route to getting love—and it's not. 99

Annabel, *Just 17 Magazine*

2a Bible scholars think that David wrote Psalm 51 after he had had a sexual affair. It expresses his sadness and asks God to forgive him. Read it for yourself. What feelings do you think David has? What does David feel now and what does he want to feel? What kind of God is being prayed to here?

2b Read Psalm 103:12. What does this say about God's attitude to sin, which includes sexual mistakes? Make this verse into a poster for a youth group.

SUMMARY
• • • • • • • • • • • • •
Christians believe that the correct place for sexual relationships is within marriage.

Making L.o.v.e

Sex is...

What is sex for? Which of the following do you agree with (a) most and (b) least?

❝ Sex is for fun. It's grown-ups' play. ❞

Jean

❝ Sex is for having children, to keep the human race going. ❞

Jonathan

❝ Sex is a way of showing that you care about somebody. ❞

Rachel

❝ Sex is for marriage. ❞

Priscilla

❝ I think sex is something very precious and intimate. Sex is so powerful and meaningful that you need to take care with it—you can cause people a lot of hurt as well as joy. ❞

Jo

❝ Making love is not an act, it's a commitment. ❞

Aaron

The majority of animals reproduce by having sex. But human beings do not just have sex in order to have children. They also refer to the act of sexual intercourse as 'making love'. What do you think they mean when they say this?

❑ **Do males and females think differently about sex?**

📁 BIBLE FILE

✚ In the Bible, 'to know' is used to mean having sexual intercourse. The biblical writers understood that in sexual intercourse a special kind of knowledge was gained. They called this 'one flesh'. It is for this reason that they taught that the correct place for sex is within a committed married relationship.

✚ Christians believe that what a person does with their body also affects their relationship with God.

1a Which of the following qualities do you think are important between two people before they make love: trust; kindness; honesty; purity; gentleness; commitment; love; faithfulness; attraction; knowledge of the other person?

1b Now prioritize these qualities putting the most important quality at the top of your list.

1c Do you think people should have sex without love?

2 What does it mean to talk about 'being in love'? Does such a state exist or is it just another description of the sex drive? What are the symptoms of 'being in love'?

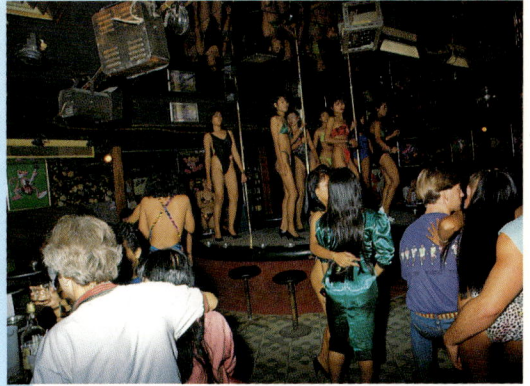

❏ **Why do Christians speak out against (a) casual sex (b) buying sex?**

Love poetry

One book in the Bible is all about romance. The Song of Songs celebrates God's gift of love and sexuality within the framework of marriage. Sex is a good thing in the correct context. Here is a taster of how the Bible celebrates love and sex:

THE WOMAN

Your lips cover me with kisses;
your love is better than wine.
There is a fragrance about you;
the sound of your name recalls it.
No woman could help loving you.
Take me with you, and we'll run away;
be my king and take me to your room.
We will be happy together,
drink deep, and lose ourselves in love.

Song of Songs 1:2–4

THE MAN

You, my love, excite men
as a mare excites the stallions of
Pharaoh's chariots.
Your hair is beautiful upon your cheeks
and falls along your neck like jewels.

Song of Songs 1:9–11

❏ **Are you surprised to find such verses in the Bible?**

What questions might each of these people be asking before they decide to make love?

Ann is a young Christian married to Mark. She explains the importance of sex in her relationship:

66 **Sexual intercourse is much more than just a physical thing. It is fun and it is also a way of celebrating our love, a way of becoming one. We bare ourselves to each other—it is a time when we can heal each other and share at the deepest level. In one word sex is a celebration. Because it is such a powerful and magical thing we believe that it has to be protected by being married.** 99

Ann, 25

SUMMARY
• • • • • • • • • • •
Christians believe that sex is a gift from God to be celebrated in a marriage relationship. It is a commitment in which a person knows another person as 'one flesh'.

The subject of abortion is controversial. Some people think it should be completely illegal since it is the killing of an unborn child. Others think that the woman should have the right to choose what happens to her own body. Every year around 140,000 women decide to have an abortion in the United Kingdom alone. It is never an easy decision to make. But what do Christians believe?

❑ **People's opinions on abortion often depend on when they think human life begins. When do you think human life begins—(a) at the moment of conception (b) on the 25th day when the heart starts beating (c) on the 28th day when the legs and arms start to form (d) at the moment of birth (e) at another time (explain when)?**

UK law allows abortion to be carried out up to the end of 24 weeks. This photo shows an unborn child at about 4 months.

❑ **Who do you think has the right to decide on abortion—(a) the mother (b) God (c) someone else (explain who)? Does the unborn child have any rights?**

The legal situation in the United Kingdom

An abortion can be legally carried out in UK if:

✔ the unborn child (fetus) is no more than 24 weeks old. After this time it is thought that a baby could be born alive and survive outside the womb.

✔ two doctors agree that it is appropriate.

✔ the pregnancy involves a risk to the physical or mental health of the mother.

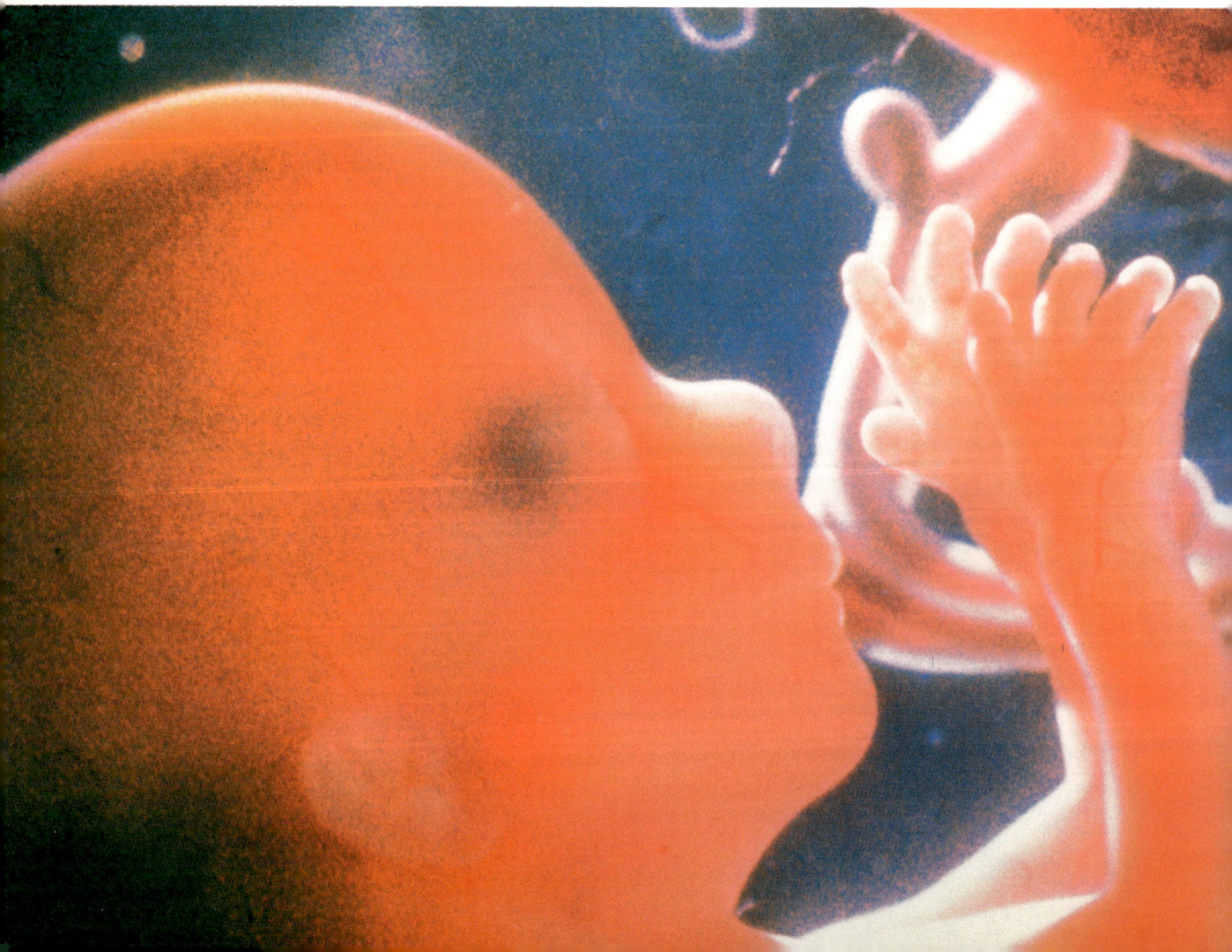

1a For some people, becoming pregnant can be very bad news. In groups, make a list of reasons people might give for wanting an abortion.

1b What do you think about these reasons—do you agree or disagree with them?

2 Choose one of the biblical statements. Design a poster to support the statement.

3 Case Study: Hayley and Laura share a flat. Hayley is pregnant after a wild party night, and is determined to have an abortion. Laura is the only one who knows. She is a Christian who thinks abortion is wrong. Hayley rejects all her pleading and her offers to find alternative help. But on the day itself, Hayley asks Laura to come with her to the abortion clinic. In groups role-play the situation and discuss what Laura should do.

4 Does a woman have a right to choose what happens to her own body? Does she have a right to choose what happens to the baby's body inside hers?

5 In groups discuss one of the following statements:

◆ The father of the unborn child has no rights to stop the abortion even if he is the husband of the mother. Why do you think this is the case? Do you think it is right? Give your reasons.

◆ By allowing abortions in the case of handicapped children we are saying 'it would be better if you were never born.' Do you think this is a right thing to say?

◆ 'The most dangerous place in the world is the human womb. Sixty million people die there every year.' (Douglas Gresham)

However, an abortion can be performed later if the mother's life or mental health is at risk or the baby will be born disabled.

Groups of people campaign on both sides of the debate.

BIBLE FILE

✚ *Each individual life is sacred.* 'God created human beings in his own image.' (Genesis 1:27)

✚ *God says that each life is precious.* 'Even if a mother should forget her child, I will never forget you. I have written your name on the palms of my hands.' (Isaiah 49:15–16) Jesus said that 'even the hairs of your head have all been counted.' (Luke 12:6)

✚ *God knows each person from the moment of conception.* When God called Jeremiah for a special job he said, 'Before I formed you in the womb I knew you; before you were born I sanctified you.' (Jeremiah 1:5; see also Psalm 139:13, 15; Isaiah 44:2, 49:1)

✚ The Bible teaches that 'You shall not murder.' (Exodus 20:13)

✚ The Bible also teaches that nothing is unforgivable; God is pictured as a loving father who wants to accept back his children who disobey his wishes. (Luke 15:11–32; Matthew 18:22)

Pro-choice

Groups such as 'The National Abortion Campaign' and 'The Abortion Rights Action League' campaign for the right of women to have abortion on demand. Why do you think they use the term 'pro-choice' and not 'pro-abortion'? What reasons do you think they use to support this position?

Pro-life

Groups such as LIFE and SPUC (The Society for the Protection of Unborn Children) provide help to women who think they are pregnant and campaign against abortions. What reasons do you think they use to support this position?

Christians have always placed a high value on human life. They have therefore spoken out against abortions.

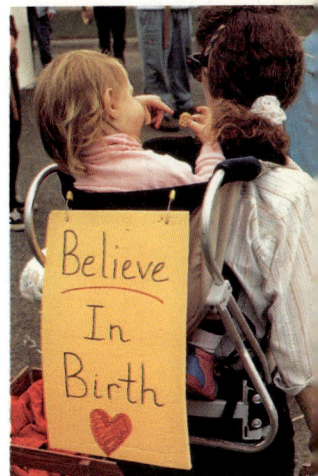

SUMMARY

Christians believe that human life is precious and must be protected at all times. Christian teaching therefore speaks out against abortion. However, Christians also believe that all people can be forgiven and given a fresh start.

❑ **Would you like to win a large amount of money on the National Lottery?**

❑ **What would you do with the money?**

❑ **Do you think it would change your life?**

Money is a very powerful and attractive thing to many people. Money can be used both for good and for bad. Sometimes it can have negative effects on your life as the following news story reports.

Money itself is not a bad thing. It all depends on what attitude you have towards it.

The story is told of a businessman who visited a monk. He told him, 'I had a dream last night telling me to come to this tree at the foot of the mountain. Here a holy man would give me a priceless stone and I would be rich for ever.' The monk reached into his bag and fetched out a jewel and handed it to the businessman. The businessman's mouth dropped in amazement of the jewel. He took the diamond and went away happy.

However, his happiness did not last long. That night he could not sleep. He wanted to plan what he would do with his new riches, but the thought of the holy man kept coming back. Before dawn, he went back to the tree and laid the diamond before the monk. And he asked, 'Please, can I have the precious gift that caused you to give away this stone?'

Adapted from *Inside Stories* by Wood and Richardson, Trentham Books

15m Family Lottery Winner
PLEASE GIVE IT BACK DAD!

The family of the father of four who scooped the 15-million lottery jackpot two weeks ago has begged him to give it back. 'It's made our lives a nightmare,' his 36-year-old wife confessed last night. 'At first we thought it was the best thing that had ever happened to us, but now I wish he hadn't won it. The pressure is unbearable and my husband is in a terrible state.'

The family is currently staying with friends and is planning to move abroad within the next few weeks to avoid further publicity.

❑ **Why was the businessman troubled? In the end did the holy man give the businessman a precious jewel which would last forever? How did he do this?**

Let me be neither rich nor poor. So give me only as much food as I need.

Proverbs 30:8

❑ **In what ways can money ruin a person's life? Why do you think the Lottery winners said that winning had made their lives a nightmare?**

What attitude towards money do you think the people in these two pictures have?

Who do you think has the healthier attitude towards money?

BRAIN ENGAGE

1 How do you use your money? What is your main priority: spending, saving or giving?

2 Read the story of the rich young man in Mark 10:17–25. How important was money to him? How can you tell? Why do you think he could not give it away? Rewrite this parable putting it in a modern-day context.

3 What do you treasure in life? What things do you set your heart on? Are they material things? Read Matthew 6:19–21. What does it say? Do you agree with it? Do you think it is possible to have money without it possessing you? Does money make you happy?

4a Watch TV adverts during the next week. How do they get you to buy their products? In what ways do adverts suggest that you would be happy if you 'just had' the latest... car, video etc.?

4b Design your own advert about money itself with the underlying message 'A good servant, a bad master'.

📁 BIBLE FILE

✚ *The Bible teaches that money can be a good thing.* 'The world and all that is in it [including money and possessions] belong to the Lord.' (Psalm 50:12) People are called to manage money wisely for God.

✚ *Possessions can possess you.* 'No one can be a slave of two masters; he will hate the one and love the other... You cannot serve both God and money.' (Matthew 6:24; see also Psalm 119:36–37) 'The love of money causes all kinds of evil.' (1 Timothy 6:10; see also Hebrews 13:5; Ecclesiastes 5:10, 6:9)

✚ *Money can blind you to the needs of others.* 'There was once a rich man who dressed in the most expensive clothes and lived in great luxury every day. There was also a poor man named Lazarus, covered with sores, who used to be brought to the rich man's door, hoping to eat the bits of food that fell from the rich man's table. Even the dogs would come and lick his sores.' (Luke 16:19–21)

SUMMARY
. . . .

Christians believe that money and possessions are a gift from God. They are on loan from God and to be used wisely to create good. They can also be dangerous if used unwisely.

Words are
Powerful

There is a rhyme which says: 'Sticks and stones may break my bones, but words can never hurt me.' Is this true?

❏ **How dangerous are words? Have you ever said something and then wished the ground would open up underneath you so you could disappear? How can words be harmful?**

❏ **Choose one of the following sayings from the Bible and draw a picture to show what you think it means, or write a story illustrating its meaning.**

Silly cow!

Think of a ship: big as it is and driven by such strong winds, it can be steered by a very small rudder, and it goes wherever the pilot wants it to go. So it is with the tongue: small as it is, it can boast about great things.

James 3:4–5

You can tame wild animals but you can't tame a tongue... The tongue runs wild, a wanton killer.

James 3:7–8

Gossip

❏ **A time for secrets. Do you ever gossip? Is gossip dangerous?**

The plucked hen

Philip Neri was a shrewd saint. Once he wanted to cure a woman of her unkind talk about others. He asked her to buy a hen for him at the market. And he told her to pluck the hen on the way back. It was a very windy day. When the woman brought the hen to Philip Neri, he complimented her and added, 'Now please leave the hen here and fetch me the feathers.'

'That is impossible,' cried the woman. 'The wind has blown them in all directions.'

Thereupon the saint said very seriously, 'And it is just as impossible to put right the bad things you say about people.'

Pierre Lefevre, *One Hundred Stories to Change Your Life*, St Pauls (UK)

BRAIN ENGAGE

1 Draw an anti-gossip poster, showing how gossip hurts its victim.

2 Newspapers often have a gossip column. Do you think it is right for them to spread unreliable bits and pieces of information about public figures? List out the benefits and disadvantages. What guidelines would you make to newspaper editors to guide their choice of what to publish?

The Bible has a lot to say about how people should speak:

✚ The tongue is a powerful tool; take care how you use it—people must control what they say. (James 3:1–12; 1 Timothy 3:11)

✚ 'Do not criticize or judge another.' (James 4:11)

✚ 'Do not use harmful words, but only helpful words, the kind that build [people] up… Get rid of bitterness, passion and anger. No more shouting or insults…' (Ephesians 4:29, 31)

✚ 'Do not accuse anyone falsely.' (Exodus 20:16)

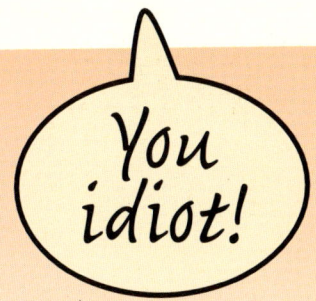

You idiot!

BRAIN ENGAGE

3 Make a list of the words people use to describe lies—for example, 'fibs', 'little white lies'. How many words have you come up with? Why do you think people use different words? Are there different types of lies?

4 Which of the following are lies?

💧 Someone tells you a joke which you don't think is funny but you laugh.

💧 A friend rings you up to ask you to go out with them tonight. You're doing nothing but you don't want to go out with them so you say you have a previous engagement.

💧 Your friend looks terrible in her new clothes but you say she looks great.

A bunch of liars

❏ **Do you lie? If so, how often—often, regularly, not often, rarely, never? Is it ever right to lie?**

According to one survey, 91% of us lie regularly. It said that we tell at least 13 major lies each week. Some people lie so often that they don't know when they are doing it! We even expect some people to lie—we are naturally suspicious of them (for example, sales people, MPs, journalists). It would appear that people are natural liars—they

what's his problem?

have a natural inclination to tell lies. Do you agree? Here are some reasons people give for telling lies:

❝ I tell lies to get out of things. ❞

Nick, 12

❝ I tell lies because it's easy. ❞

Sam, 16

❝ Sometimes I tell lies because to tell the truth would hurt somebody. ❞

Tony, 14

Get a life!

❏ **What other reasons can you think of?**

❏ **Have you ever told a lie for any of the above reasons?**

❏ **Are some of the reasons better than others? Explain your answer.**

❏ **Is it ever right to tell a lie?**

SUMMARY
Christians believe that they should love their neighbour, and take care when they speak to others and especially when they speak about others.

29

Why do people suffer?

Everyone suffers at one time or another during their life. When you look at the world around you, it can seem full of suffering.

❏ **What types of suffering are described in the following newspaper headlines?**

❏ **What questions do the pictures raise in your mind?**

❏ **What has caused the suffering? Is it caused by humans or has it some natural cause?**

AIDS e claims further m ev

Earthquake rocks southern Turkey

Famine adds to the problems of refugees

Some of the suffering we see around us is clearly caused by what people do, carelessly, selfishly or maliciously. However, sometimes suffering is caused by factors outside people's control (for example earthquakes and famines), and there appears

📁 BIBLE FILE

The Bible gives clues as to why suffering came into the world. The story of God creating a world that is good is told in the first two chapters of the Bible. However, the third chapter describes how people rebelled against God and are forced to bear the consequences—conflict, suffering and death.

Jesus develops this teaching when he says: 'From the inside, from a person's heart, come the evil ideas which lead him to do immoral things, to rob, kill, commit adultery, be greedy, and do all sorts of evil things.' (Mark 7:21)

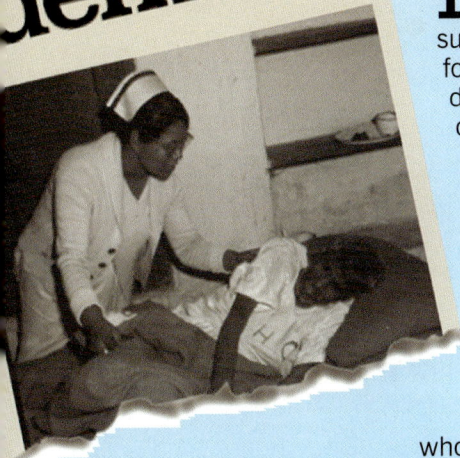

demic

1 Draw a table with two columns—one for suffering caused by nature and another for suffering caused by humans. Write the following forms of suffering under the correct column: disasters caused by volcanoes, floods, AIDS, death by road accident, starvation, physical handicaps. Do any of the following fall under both? Explain why. Add three other forms of suffering under each column.

2a Watch two TV programmes, one of which should be the news. Make a list of all the forms of suffering mentioned.

2b Design a 'first-aid' plan to help people who are suffering. Suggest what people can do to meet the needs of these people who are suffering.

3 Write a letter of complaint to God in which you confront him with all the suffering in the world.

4 Some people say that there cannot be a God if there is so much suffering. What do you think?

In units 29–41 we will be exploring questions which affect the world as a whole—for example: Why are some people rich and others so poor? What is happening to the earth? You will be invited to consider what you can do about these issues. You will be exploring Christian beliefs and values in relation to these issues.

One of the themes running through these units will be the suffering which people in all different situations have to endure, and also the way in which planet earth is suffering due to pollution. Units 29–32 introduce you to some of the religious ideas involved in the whole section.

to be no clear reason for it. It is at these times that people cannot help but ask what is happening.

For some people, the existence of suffering, and in particular suffering which has not been caused by humans, is the main reason why they find it difficult to believe in God and for disliking religion altogether.

One teenager who finds it difficult to believe in God wrote this:

66 It seems cowardly to both attack God for the existence of suffering whilst at the same time not quite believing in him with my heart. One must believe in God before one can pin the blame on him, and in the process of coming to believe in him the need to pin the blame lessens. I'm not saying that if I believed in God, life would suddenly become so much more understandable, but I think I would be able to trust enough that understanding wouldn't be so essential. I would feel safe in the belief that I can never see things as God sees them, that I can't understand everything. **99**

Nick, 17

❏ **What is Nick trying to say in the quote on the left? Do you agree with him?**

66 Bad things happen in the world when good people remain silent. 99

❏ **Is this true?**

SUMMARY
The existence of suffering is for some people the greatest obstacle to belief in God. As you explore the issues raised in units 33–41 you will need to ask yourself where God might stand in relation to the suffering in the world.

30

Evil and Suffering

Sometimes suffering is so horrible that the word 'evil' is used to describe it. The murdering of millions of people in the Second World War (including Jews, gypsies, homosexuals) by Hitler is one example. This word has also been used of the murderer Frederick West.

26TH NOVEMBER 1995

PARTNERS IN EVIL

SERIAL KILLERS MURDER TWELVE WOMEN IN HOUSE OF HORROR

In the house and rear garden of 25 Cromwell Street, the police recovered the remains of twelve young women, one of whom was Frederick West's eldest daughter, Heather. Each body had bones missing: seven had lost neck bones, seven were missing kneecaps and the skeleton of one was without a shoulder bone. All these things pointed to cannibalism.

The police had been interested in the family for some time. Fred was accused of having sexual intercourse with one or more of his daughters while being encouraged by his wife. He also used to bring prostitutes home for his wife. During interrogation it was found that Rosemary West used to save some of the sperm from her lovers and inject it into one of her daughters to try to make her pregnant.

When the bodies were discovered a leading forensic psychologist commented that, 'They didn't just kill for the sake of taking a life; their victims were playthings who were tortured and abused.' What was it within their lives that gave them the need to torture, rape and kill a string of young women? In many ways, Rosemary and Frederick West are no different from the rest of us. They were, by most accounts, outwardly friendly and good neighbours. Frederick carried on with his life—working, drinking with his mates. He doesn't feel sorry: the word means nothing to him. In prison he told his son, Stephen West, that he could not stop what he was doing.

The file on Frederick and Rosemary West cannot be closed because there are more victims to be found.

Adapted from an article by Paul Britton, *The Sunday Times*, 26 November 1995

What makes people do bad things?

Christians believe that God created people with free will to choose between right and wrong. They believe that the source of evil, the Devil, encouraged people to rebel (see unit 13). As a consequence, the world has departed from God's original perfect design for it.

As one teenager commented:

66 Since we can choose between good and evil, God cannot come in and make us do good. He is not a dictator. In the same way, God cannot come in and fix everything that's wrong with this world. 99

Basem, 17

In unit 6, we saw how Christians believe that we are born with a bias towards doing what is wrong which causes other people to suffer.

Brain Engage

1a What is your first reaction to the 'Partners in Evil' story? Is it (i) to punish them (ii) to try to understand why they did it (iii) to forgive them?

1b How do you react to things you do wrong, when you fail to live up to ideals? Do you (i) try to understand why you do things wrong (ii) forgive yourself (iii) punish yourself (iv) make a determined effort to change? Which do you think is the most responsible response?

1c What do you think is the Christian response to (i) the case of Frederick West (ii) yourself when you do things wrong?

2 Look at Monique's opinion (on the right). Do you agree that people are born with a bias to do wrong? What do you think the mother of a newborn baby would reply to Monique?

3a Do you think 'evil' is a correct word to use for Frederick and Rosemary West? What makes what they did 'evil' as opposed to just 'bad'? Do you think we are all capable of doing what Frederick and Rosemary West did? If not, what stops us?

3b What do you think Frederick West meant when he told his son that he could not stop what he was doing?

Prisoners in a concentration camp during the Second World War

> **66** I can remember very well people of ex-Yugoslavia—people like me, men who were friends of mine, who went out and did terrible things, killing others. But they are the same people who offered me water-melon on the beach when I was a child. How could they have changed so much? It is for this reason that I believe each of us has the potential to do evil things. You can see this in small children. They can be more cruel with each other than adults. **99**

Monique, 18

Christians believe that all people fall short of the perfect ideal for us but that some rebel against God so completely that they become evil. However, they also believe that all people, even people like Hitler and Frederick West, can be rescued by God and given a fresh start if they turn away from their sins—the Bible says, 'There is nothing… that will ever be able to separate us from the love of God.' (Romans 8:38) Christians are called to forgive their enemies.

War does not respect personal belongings. How would you feel towards people who had destroyed your house and all your possessions?

Summary
One Christian response to explain suffering is the belief that the Devil tempts people to do evil things to others.

31

Where is God in the midst of suffering?

❑ **Where is God in the midst of suffering? What kind of God is it that allows people to suffer? Does God care?**

Have you ever asked these questions? If so, you are not alone. People have struggled with them for centuries. The Bible records a number of people who have demanded of God an explanation for all the suffering in the world. For example, King David had trouble understanding where God was in times of need. In one of his psalms he cries out, 'My God, my God, why have you forsaken me? Why are you so far from saving me?' Sometimes it's hard to understand what God is doing in the world. Is God absent? Doesn't he have the power to control things?

In this unit you will be examining a number of beliefs which Christians have about God and suffering.

God suffers with people

Christians believe that God understands our suffering. For example, Jesus, God's Son, suffered at the hands of both his friends and enemies.

Mathias Grünewald painted this picture of Jesus' crucifixion for the chapel of a hospital for plague victims in Isenheim, 1513–1515. What words come to mind when you look at this painting? Why do you think Grünewald painted the crucifixion like this for a plague hospital? If you had to give this painting a title, what would it be?

❝ **God created people with free will. God shares in the agony of people's suffering like a mother watching her druggie son destroy his own life. The love of God is suffering love.** ❞

James, 16

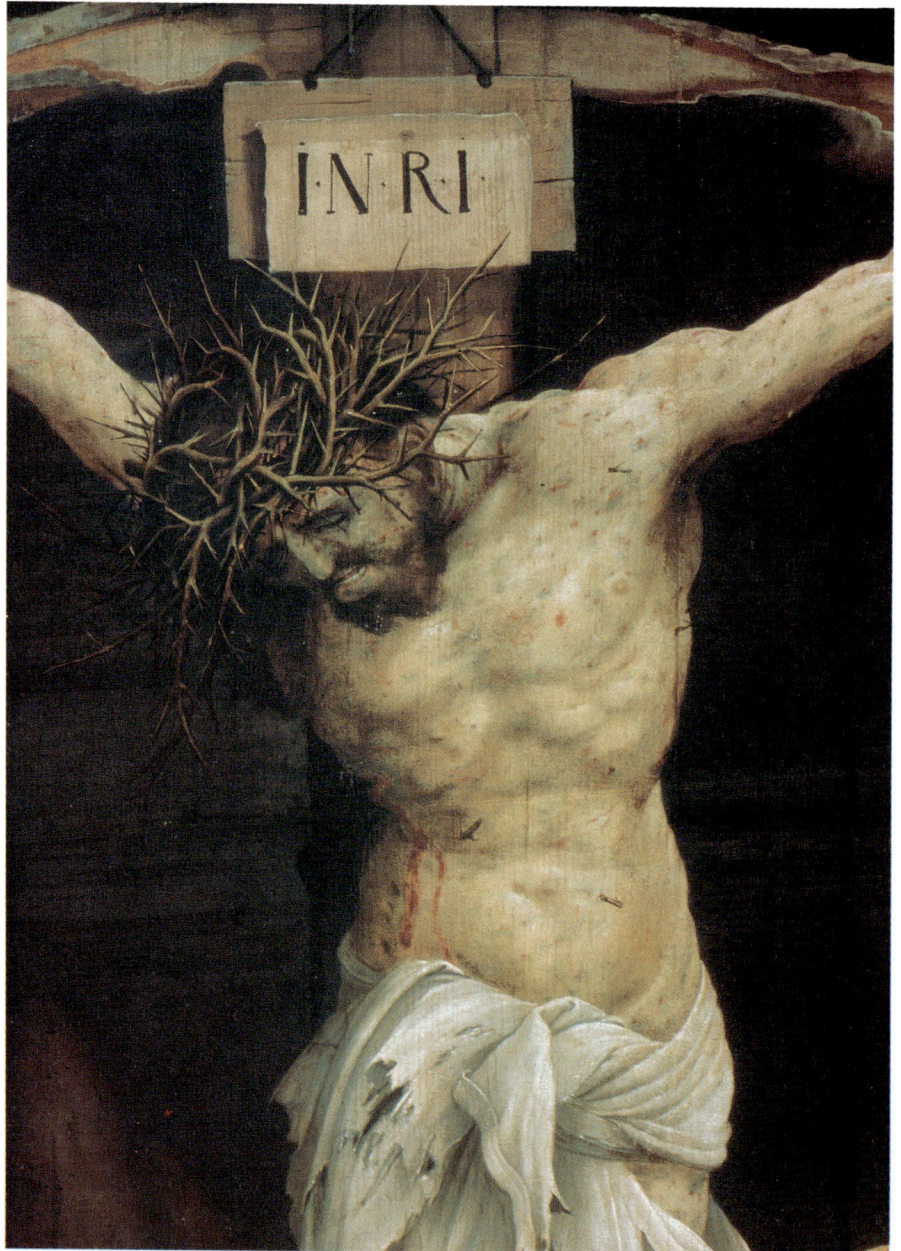

God supports people in their suffering

In unit 7 we looked at the Christian belief that God sent his Son, Jesus, to rescue and help people. Many Christians speak of the real help God gives them in times of great need. They do not always escape trouble, but they are confident of God's support, as the following story attempts to explain.

Footprints

One night a man had a dream. He dreamt he was walking along the beach with the Lord. Across the sky flashed scenes from his life. For each scene he noticed two sets of footprints in the sand: one belonging to him, and the other to the Lord.

When the last scene of his life flashed before him, he looked back at the footprints in the sand. He noticed that many times along the path of his life there was only one set of footprints. He also noticed that it happened at the very lowest and saddest times in his life.

This really bothered him and he questioned the Lord about it. 'Lord, you said that once I decided to follow you, you'd walk with me all the way. But I have noticed that during the most troublesome times in my life, there is only one set of footprints. I don't understand why when I needed you most you would leave me.'

The Lord replied, 'My precious, precious child, I love you and I would never leave you. During your times of trial and suffering, when you see only one set of footprints, it was then that I carried you.'

BRAIN ENGAGE

1 The account of Jesus' crucifixion can be found at the end of all four Gospels. Read one account and list all the forms of suffering Jesus underwent.

2a Imagine that you have a brother or sister who is suffering through their addiction to drugs or drink. Write a diary account expressing your feelings of helplessness and how you suffer to watch them.

2b How does this help you to understand how God suffers with his creation?

3 Think of a type of suffering you have to face alone—exams, dental treatment or worse! Imagine that a good friend has offered to support you in any way they can. Write a list of things you would like them to do. Discuss how a supportive friend helps.

God is in control

In spite of all the suffering in the world, Christians believe that God is in control. He alone knows the reason for suffering.

> 66 Life is like a patchwork quilt: we see only the ragged, ugly side, while God sees the beautiful pattern on the other side. 99
>
> Ann

SUMMARY

Christians believe in a God who understands what suffering is because he has also suffered in the person of Jesus. However, God created people out of love and with freedom of choice. This means that God will not intervene in every case to stop people from suffering.

32

Why did it have to happen?

❑ **Do you think any good can come out of suffering? In groups, share experiences of suffering and any positive benefits it has had.**

Some people believe that there is no purpose in suffering—it is just meaningless. Christians, however, believe that God can use our suffering to help us to grow as people. This does not mean that they believe suffering is good, but that it does not have the ultimate power to destroy.

Suffering, the teacher

Some people believe we can use suffering to teach us lessons.

66 I believe God does not like people to suffer but he wants to work with people in their suffering to help them grow. I like to compare it with the process of turning iron ore into steel. The iron begins in the rock and as such is useless for any purpose. However, when it is mixed with some limestone and heated to an intense degree it is separated from its impurities. Now you have iron, but it is still not totally useful. Therefore it is put back into the oven and heated again. When it cools it is steel. Such is the case with people. God is active in our lives.

Suffering can be used by God to refine us although God doesn't actually cause us to suffer in the first place. 99

Abel, 17

At 17, Joni Eareckson broke her neck in a diving accident and was totally paralysed from the neck down. The fun-filled life she enjoyed was blighted, and she suffered enormously in the months of recovery and the years of learning how to function as a quadriplegic. Yet gradually she learned new and good things: about her own talents as a writer and artist; about the courage and compassion of others; and about how God could help and encourage her, even though she was not physically 'cured'.

Suffering as a warning

Some pain and suffering can serve the useful purpose of warning us that something is wrong. For example, without toothache we would not realize that our teeth and gums were in need of treatment. Make a list of other occasions in which suffering can act as a warning that something is wrong. What about non-physical examples such as in relationships?

Like suffering, the smelting and refining of a metal is a costly process designed to remove impurities.

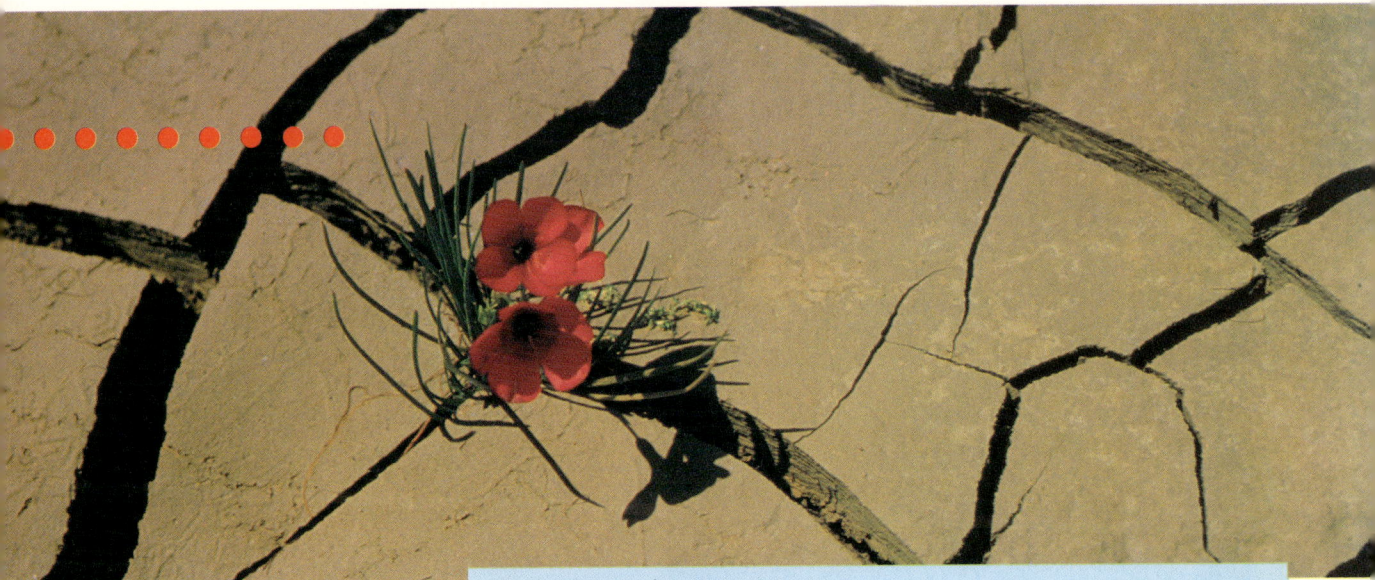

A beautiful flower can grow out of barren soil. How might you relate this image to the experiences of the cancer victim below?

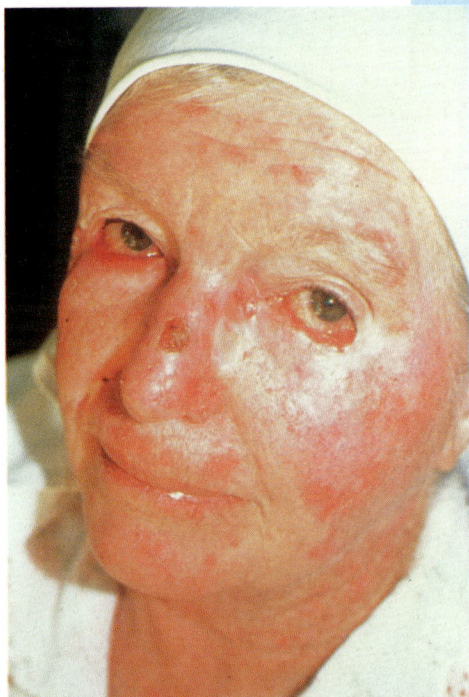

BRAIN ENGAGE

1 Read the following passages from the Bible: James 1:2–4; Romans 5:3–5. Match them with the following statements: (i) Suffering helps to develop your character (ii) Suffering helps a person's faith to grow (iii) Suffering helps you to become mature.

2 If suffering is a learning process, what do you think are the lessons which are being taught? Could these lessons be learnt without suffering?

3 In the Second World War, many Jews suffered at the hands of the Nazis in concentration and death camps. In their dormitories, some Jews placed a chair in the middle of their bunks for God. They put God on trial asking him to explain why he had allowed so much suffering. In pairs, one of you choose to be the counsel for God's defence and the other for his prosecution. Using the last four units, write out your speeches either defending God or prosecuting him. Read these out to the class.

4 Discuss: 'Would the world be a better or worse place without suffering?'

makes us perfect. We think our childish toys bring us all the happiness that there is and our nursery is the whole wide world. But something must drive us out of the nursery to the world of others. And that something is suffering.

As taken from the film 'Shadowlands'

Suffering broadens our life experience

C.S. Lewis wrote the following whilst watching his wife die of cancer:

Pain is God's megaphone to rouse a deaf world. We are like blocks of stone out of which the sculptor carves the forms of men. The blows of his chisel which hurt us so much are what

SUMMARY
Christians believe that suffering can be given a meaning—people can grow through times of suffering. They also believe that in God's future there will be no more suffering.

33

Justice

It's not fair!

❏ **Work in pairs. Try to describe an occasion when you felt you were unjustly treated. What happened? How did you feel?**

❏ **What do you do when you are treated unfairly or when others are treated unfairly? Do you speak out?**

How many of you chose an incident to do with school—for example getting told off for something you did not do, but you were in the wrong place at the wrong time? Why do some people get away with doing the most amazing things wrong—they never seem to get caught?

Sometimes the whole of a person's life may seem unfair—for example, why are some people born into rich families and others into families which are starving because of a natural disaster?

As you look around the world, you can see example after example of things which are unjust. It is quite natural to ask why, and for those who believe in God to ask, 'Where is God in all of this?', 'Which side is God on?'

Christians believe that God is a just and fair God who wants people to act justly with each other.

If you oppress poor people, you insult the God who made them; but kindness shown to the poor is an act of worship.

Proverbs 14:31

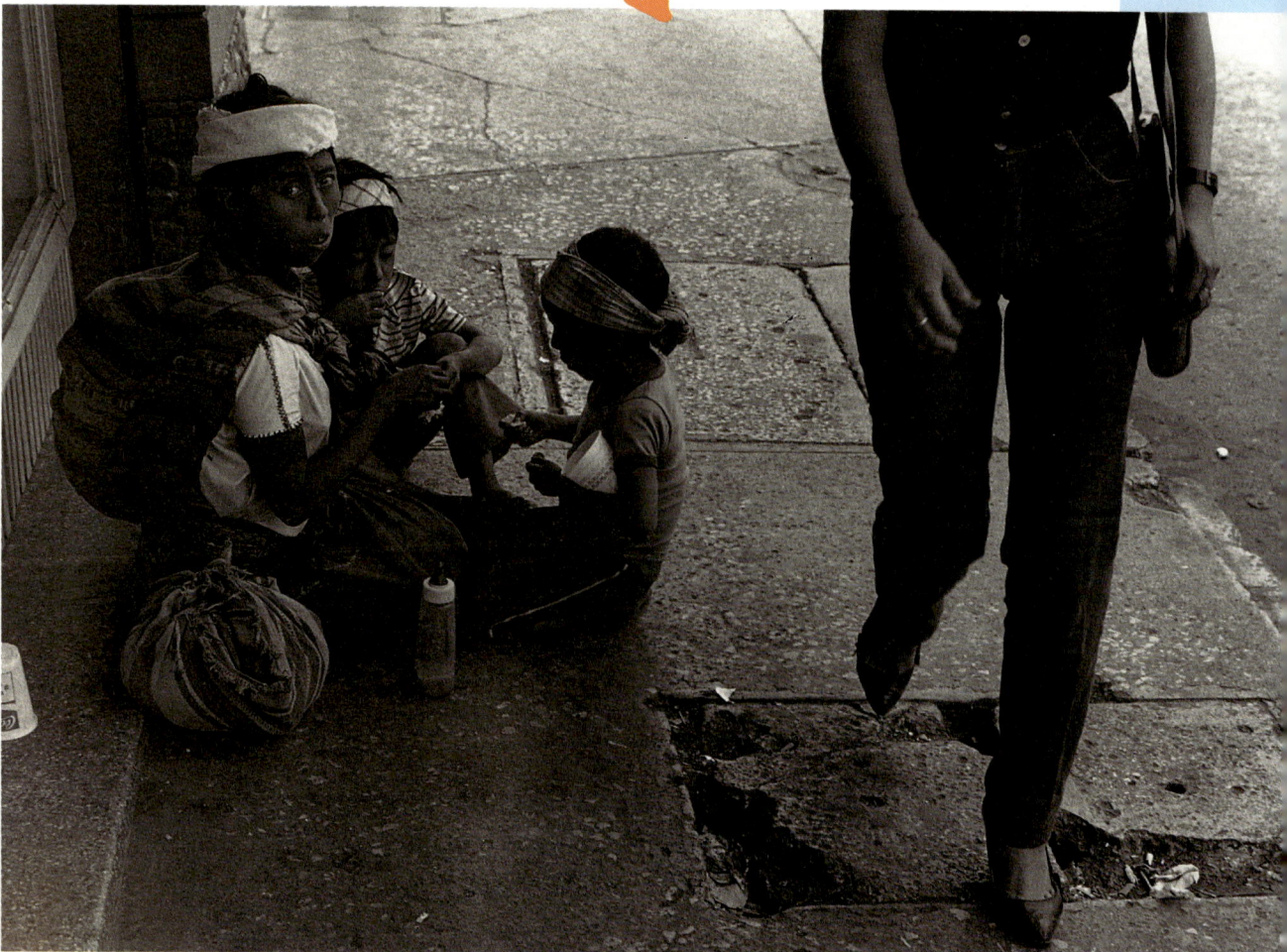

As You Did It to The Least Of These…

Remember the poor when you look out
on fields you own,
on your plump cows grazing.
Remember the poor when you look into
your barn
at the abundance
of the harvest.
Remember the
poor when the
wind howls
and the rain falls,
as you sit warm
in your dry
house…
The poor have no
food except what you feed them
no shelter except your house
when you welcome them,
no warmth except your glowing fire.

Robert Van de Weyer, *Celtic Fire*, Doubleday

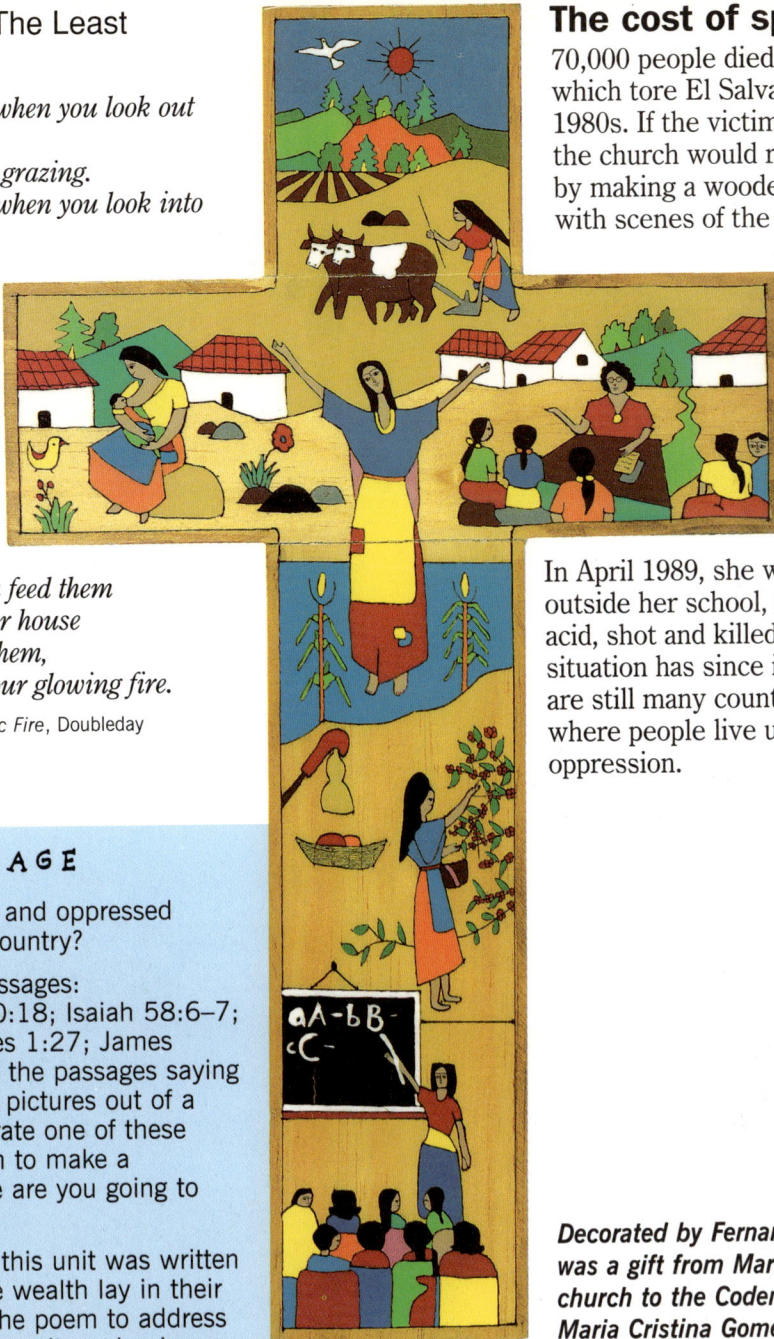

BRAIN ENGAGE

1 Are there poor and oppressed people in your country?

2 Read these passages: Deuteronomy 10:18; Isaiah 58:6–7; Psalm 103:6; James 1:27; James 2:14–16. What are the passages saying about God? Choose pictures out of a newspaper to illustrate one of these passages. Use them to make a montage. What title are you going to give it?

3a The poem in this unit was written to people whose wealth lay in their farmland. Rewrite the poem to address people in your community, using images from the way they make a living.

3b Try writing a poem which deals with another area of injustice—for example people who are unjustly in prison or people who are discriminated against because of their beliefs or their ethnic background.

4 What does the cross tell you about Maria Cristina Gomez? In groups, make your own cross which depicts your lives and concerns—you may like to include concerns you have about your own life, your town, your country, or even worldwide concerns such as the mistreatment of animals or other human beings.

The cost of speaking out

70,000 people died in the civil war which tore El Salvador apart in the 1980s. If the victim was a Christian, the church would remember them by making a wooden cross decorated with scenes of the person's life, showing things which had been important to that person.

This is the cross of Maria Cristina Gomez—she was a Christian school teacher.

In April 1989, she was kidnapped outside her school, tortured with acid, shot and killed. Although the situation has since improved, there are still many countries in the world where people live under injustice and oppression.

Decorated by Fernando Llort, the cross was a gift from Maria's family and church to the Codena de la Esperanza Maria Cristina Gomez.

SUMMARY
• • • • • • • • • • • • •
Christians believe that God is a just God. Christians should speak out against all forms of injustice. God is on the side of all those who are oppressed, whether it is by poverty, violence or injustice.

34

Fighting Injustice

What is happening in each of these photographs? Imagine that you were the editor of a newspaper. Give each one a snappy caption.

If you were asked to choose two pictures to show acts of injustice which you know about, what would they be?

Sleeping on the streets

In the last unit we looked at the Christian belief that God was on the side of people who were being oppressed. This unit will look at Christian responses to injustice.

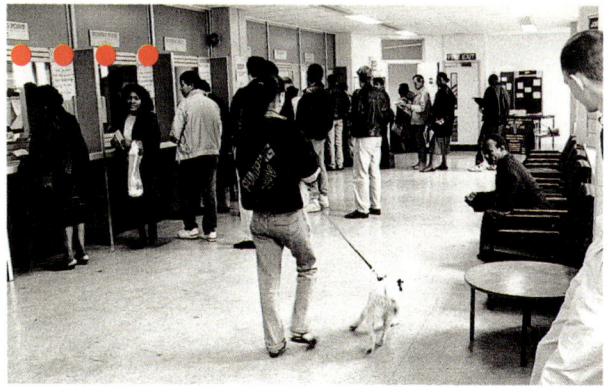

Queues at a London dole office

Speaking out

Within Christianity there has always been a tradition of people speaking out against injustice. One example of this has been the role of liberation theology in Asia, Latin America and South Africa in this century. The Church has taken a positive option to stand with the poor against all powers and governments which try to keep them poor. Many clergy, nuns and lay people have chosen to live and work with poor communities in the attempt to free people from injustice, violence and poverty. Each time life for the poor is improved and justice is restored, Christians believe that God's kingdom is brought into the world.

Liberation theology is about working for justice in shanty towns like this.

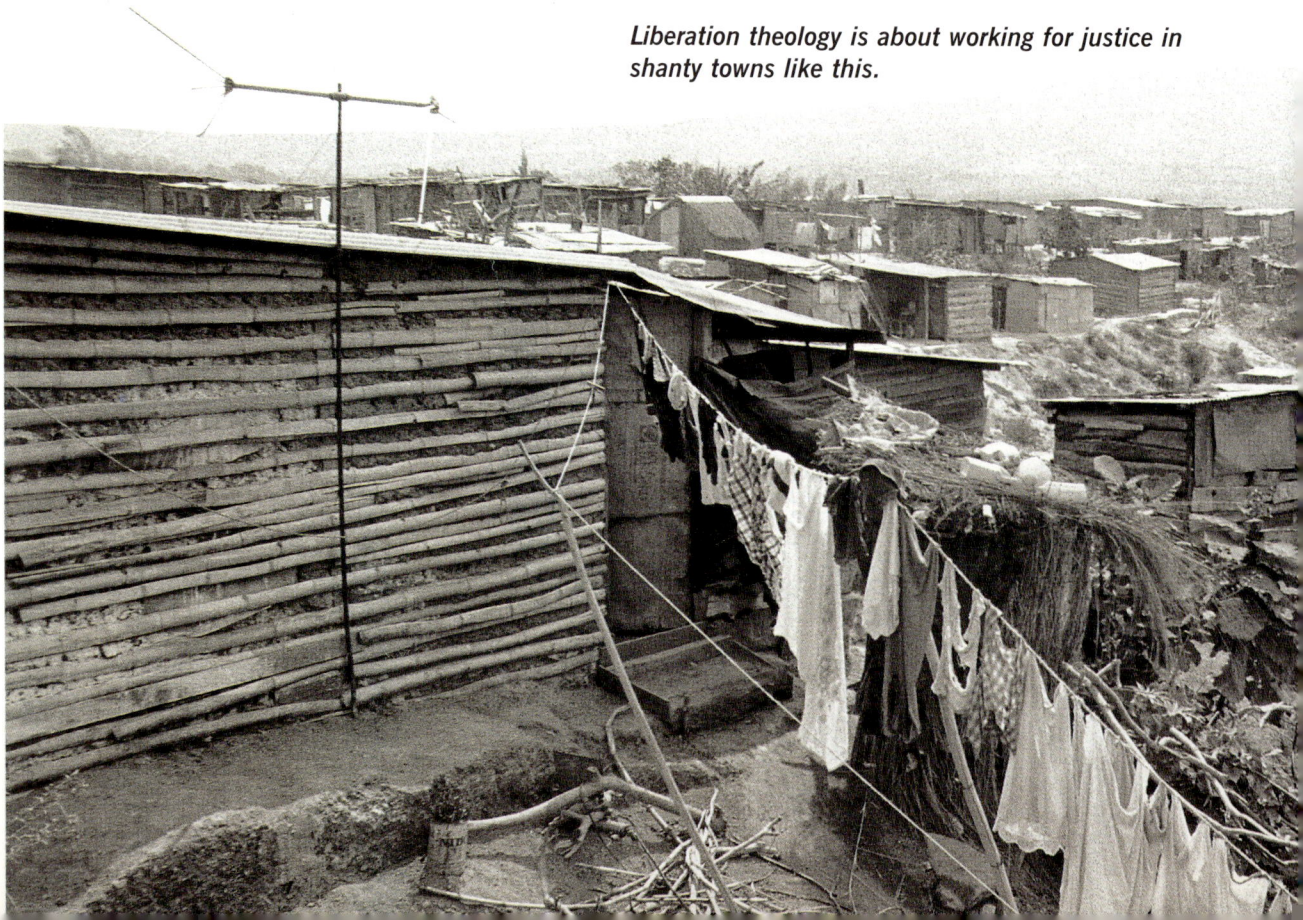

✠ All people were made in God's image (Genesis 1:27) and therefore each individual person is important in God's eyes, not to be abused. Their human rights are to be protected.

✠ People are called to love each other as neighbours. (Mark 12:31) Each person is responsible for others.

✠ Throughout the Bible, God appears as the liberator who frees the oppressed. 'God who does what is right is always on the side of the oppressed.' (Psalm 103:6; see also Psalm 146:7–9)

✠ God demands justice. God's prophets continually call people to act justly with each other. (Isaiah 61:1–2, 8)

66 Christians and all those who hate injustice are obliged to fight it with every ounce of their strength. They must work for a new world in which greed and selfishness will finally be overcome. 99

Ignacio Ellacuria, one of six Jesuit priests murdered for their support of the poor in El Salvador in November 1989

Forgiveness

Christianity teaches that all wrongdoers can be forgiven for what they have done. Christians would therefore agree with the words of the following prayer which was found scribbled on a piece of wrapping paper near the body of a child at Ravensbruck concentration camp.

O Lord,
remember not only the men and women
of good will
but also those of evil will.
But do not remember all the suffering
they have inflicted upon us;
remember the fruits we have borne
thanks to this suffering—
our comradeship, our loyalty, our humility,
our courage, our generosity,
the greatness of heart
which has grown out of all this;
and when they come to the judgement,
let all the fruits that we have borne
be their forgiveness.

When Jesus was on the cross, he cried out to God to forgive the people who were killing him—'Father, forgive them, for they know not what they do.'

BRAIN ENGAGE

1 During the next week, read through a selection of newspapers. Make up your own scrapbook on human rights—where they are being kept and where they are being ignored. Are any of the human rights being denied in your country?

2 Why do you think Christians should be involved in working for human rights?

3 Imagine that you were in charge of designing a campaign to raise people's consciousness about the violation of human rights in the world. The motto for your campaign is 'Building Moral Outrage'. In groups plan your campaign. What activities could you do? What advertising would you need? How are you going to promote your campaign?

SUMMARY
• • • • • • • • • •
Christians believe that because all people are made in God's image, every individual is important and equal. Each person deserves justice. Christians are also called to forgive and to work towards a world in which justice and peace will reign.

35

Prejudice

How does the way you see people affect how you treat them? For example, what words come to your mind when you look at the following photographs?

❑ **What do these people have in common? How do they differ?**

❑ **Do you think that some people are more valuable than others?**

❑ **Which do you think is the best to be treasurer of a club?**

The word 'prejudice' means to prejudge somebody or something before you really know them. If you are prejudiced against something or someone, you have an unreasonable dislike of them. If you then act upon these feelings of dislike you *discriminate* against the person or thing. People can be discriminated against in many ways, for example, by being bullied, not offered jobs or housing.

Prejudice expresses itself in a number of ways. We shall look at two of these ways in this unit.

1 Racism

Racism is the belief that people of some races are inferior to others.

Collins Cobuild English Dictionary

These people are then treated as second-class citizens.

❑ **In the Second World War the Nazis treated the Jews as inferior and killed 6 million Jews in extermination camps. Do you think the same thing could happen today to a race?**

❑ **The 1992 British Crime Survey estimated that there are between 130,000 and 140,000 racial attacks a year.**

❝ **The Christian faith teaches that every member of the human race is a child of God, so a Christian is not free to be a racist.** ❞

Richard Holloway, *Paradoxes of Christian Faith and Life*, Mowbray

❝ **The most horrible aspect of apartheid, a blasphemous aspect, is that it can make a child of God doubt they are a child of God.** ❞

Desmond Tutu

Black or white?

2 Sexism

Sexism is the belief that the members of one sex, usually women, are less intelligent or less capable than those of the other sex and need not be treated equally.

Collins Cobuild English Dictionary

Over the last thirty years women's rights have been greatly discussed in public.

Which of the following are sexist? Explain your choice:

❏ Paying a woman less than a man for the same job.

❏ Reproaching a man for not knowing how to do household repairs.

❏ Expecting a woman to do all the household chores.

❏ Sniggering at a man who chooses a non-traditionally male hobby—e.g. flower arranging.

❏ Calling a woman 'love' or 'dear'.

BRAIN ENGAGE

1 Explain the following words and illustrate them by providing an example for each: prejudice; discrimination.

2 Which groups of people today are discriminated against? For example, you may like to think if, and how, children are discriminated against.

3 A Nigerian student wrote: 'God is black, a beautiful shining black. It is a wicked white man's lie to say that he is white. The Devil is white.' What is this student trying to say? What do you think he means when he says that the Devil is white?

4 The language we use is often sexist—we talk about mankind, manpower, craftsmen. Some people have thought that we should change all references to God as male in the Bible. Do you agree?

5 Discuss the following quotes:

66 We believe that for years women have been victims of sexual violence and harassment. They have been treated as sex objects by the advertisement business. 99

66 Mothers should be paid for staying at home and caring for their children. 99

66 Men and women are equal but have different roles in life. 99

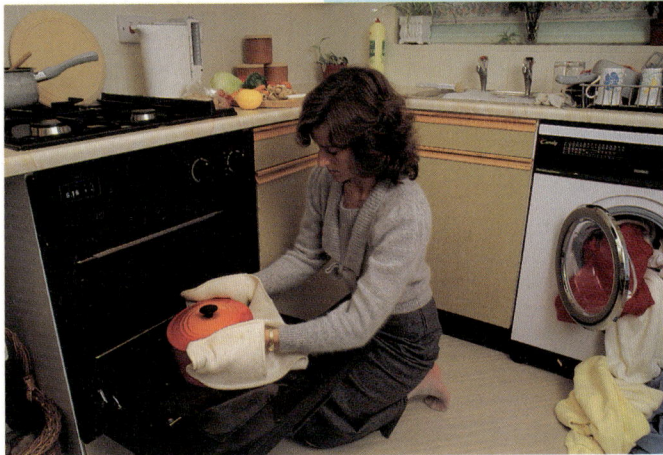

36

Who is my neighbour?

❑ **List as many differences as you can between the two families in the photographs on this page.**

❑ **In groups brainstorm a list of reasons to account for these differences.**

If you look at the distribution of the earth's resources you could easily say, 'It's not fair!' Imagine that there are thirty people in your class at the moment and that the classroom represented the world. What would your scaled-down 'world' be like?

Did you know...?

✘ Only two of you would live to the age of 74.

✘ Two of you would be so underfed that it would prevent you from growing properly.

✘ 17 of you would make less than £300 a year.

✘ Only 15 of you would be able to get clean drinking water.

✘ One of you would control 80% of the farmland.

✘ Only six of you would live in safe homes.

Adapted from *Youth Bible*, Word Publishing

❑ **What reasons can you suggest for the world not being fair?**

Statistics suggest that about 1.2 billion people today live without sufficient food, clothing and shelter to meet their basic needs.

The economist Robert Heilbroner said that the following things would have to be ripped out of a modern house to turn it into a Developing World family home: chairs, beds, tables, clothes, kitchen appliances, nearly all the food, all the taps, bath, loos, all electricity.

Then he adds, 'Next we take away the house. The family can move to the toolshed.' What is left: a few blankets, a table, a wooden chair, one set of your oldest clothes, a pair of shoes for your dad (but for no one else), a small bag of flour, sugar and salt.

BIBLE FILE

✠ Jesus himself said that whatever you do to one another you do also to him. (Matthew 25:40; see also the parable of the Good Samaritan—Luke 10:25–37)

✠ Jesus told his disciples to 'Love your neighbour as you love yourself.' (Matthew 22:39) The Bible explains that the love of other people is a good way of seeing how much you love God. (1 John 4:20–21)

✠ This love must result in action. (1 John 3:17–18)

You may find it useful to look at the unit on money (unit 27) for Christian attitudes to wealth.

BRAIN ENGAGE

1 Imagine what it would be like to wake up one morning and find that overnight you had become a poor villager in the Developing World. What differences would you notice? Write a diary extract for the day.

2 Design a church poster presenting a Christian message about the unequal distribution of the earth's resources. You may like to consider one of the following issues:

♦ What does the Bible say about the relationship between people as neighbours?

♦ How do you think a Christian is to live in a rich society?

♦ What should they do with their own money?

♦ Is it OK to buy luxuries?

♦ How should they treat people who do spend money on their own luxuries?

EXTRA

3a During the next week, keep an account of how much money you spend on having 'fun' (for example, eating out, going to the cinema, buying sweets, renting videos).

3b Research what that money might have bought if given to a charity organisation such as OXFAM.

4 Giving money to a needy person can be one way of helping them. Think of the difference you might make to people in your community if you were prepared to…

♦ Give up 1–2 hours a week to do some form of voluntary work.

♦ Take time to chat to people you meet.

♦ Invite someone with few friends to join you for a meal.

❏ **Countries of the northern hemisphere use four fifths of the world's resources even though only one fifth of the world's population lives there. Is it only thieves who steal or are we stealing from people in developing countries by being unwilling to share?**

Christians believe that each person is a neighbour to each other since we all belong to God's family. In today's world, modern technology allows us to know what is happening in most parts of the world within seconds. We all belong together. At the most practical levels, it is possible to treat all the people of the world as our neighbours.

66 God hides under the appearance of one's neighbour—and this is the approach which he probably uses most in the modern world. 99

Michel Quoist, *Meet Christ and Live*, Gill and Macmillan

SUMMARY
• • • • • • • • • • • •
Christians believe that all people are made and valued by God—each person is a neighbour to each other.

37

What Happens When I Do Things Wrong?

❏ **What is happening in each of these pictures?**

❏ **What do you think is a suitable response to the person? Is punishment a good idea?**

❏ **Is it important to know a person's motives for doing something wrong? Would this make a difference to how you responded to them? Try to give an example.**

❏ When society punishes people, it could be trying to do a number of things:

✘ To protect society from somebody's bad behaviour.

✘ To put other people off from behaving wrongly.

✘ To reform the person who has done wrong— to make them a better person.

✘ To punish somebody for what they have done.

Christians take into account two main ideas when considering how to respond to people who have done things wrong. The first is that God is just and will see that justice be done.

There was once a king who decided to check on his servants' accounts. He had begun to do so when a servant was brought in who owed him millions of pounds. The servant did not have enough money to pay his debt, so the king ordered him and his family to be sold into slavery to raise the money. The servant fell on his knees and begged him for mercy. The king felt sorry for him, released him from his debt and let him go.

Then the man went out and met one of his fellow servants who owed him a couple of pounds. He grabbed him and demanded that he be paid. His fellow servant fell on his knees and pleaded with him for mercy. He refused.

When the king heard what had happened he was very angry and sent for his servant. He told the servant that he should have shown the same mercy as was shown to him. Then he sent the servant to jail until he could pay back the full amount that he owed the king.

Matthew 18:21–35

BIBLE FILE

✚ In order to stop unjust revenge and to encourage fair punishment, the Old Testament rule was 'If anyone injures another person, whatever he has done shall be done to him.' (Leviticus 24:19)

✚ Jesus went further and taught the rule of forgiveness: 'You have heard that it was said, "An eye for an eye, and a tooth for a tooth." But now I tell you: do not take revenge on someone who wrongs you... love your enemies and pray for those who persecute you.' (Matthew 5:38–39, 43)
In the prayer which Jesus taught his disciples he said, 'Forgive us the wrongs we have done, as we forgive the wrongs that others have done to us.' (Matthew 6:12)

1 Imagine that you are the form teacher of Year 9. Virtually every day you are getting complaints from other teachers about Tom and Jeff.

♦ Since Tom's parents split up 8 months ago, he has been getting into more and more trouble at school. He can't settle in class, does not always do his homework and is starting to get into fights in the school yard.

♦ Although Jeff is never the one to actually get into trouble, he taunts and dares his friends to do silly things. He stirs and creates rumours so that other people get into trouble.

As a Christian teacher, what do you do? Do you treat each the same and therefore appear to be fair or do you treat them differently? Explain your action.

2 Read the account of Jesus' meeting with the woman who had been caught in adultery. (John 8:1–11) What was the normal punishment for committing adultery (verse 5)? How did Jesus reply to the teachers of the law? What did he say to the woman (verses 10–11)? Did Jesus punish her? Do you think she would commit adultery again? What do you think Jesus' response would be if she did?

3a Consider the four reasons society gives for putting criminals in jail. In groups, discuss which is the (i) most Christian and (ii) least Christian response. Give your reasons.

3b Can and should one forgive someone who has not apparently repented? Can forgiveness be combined with a just punishment?

❝ **Forgiveness is the refusal to pay back evil with evil. 'Forgive and forget' is no Christian slogan. 'Remember and forgive' is. For Christians, Jesus set the pattern in praying for his own executioners: 'Father forgive them…' This was the response of Gordon Wilson when IRA killers murdered his daughter. This was the response of Dr Sheila Cassidy to her Chilean torturers.** ❞

Paul Oestreicher, Letter to The Editor, *The Times*, 22 January 1996

The second is the Christian belief that God is also forgiving and is willing to welcome anyone back who admits their wrongdoing and asks God's forgiveness. The emphasis is very much on waiting for God's justice and offering forgiveness.

In the story of the runaway son (Luke 15:11–32), God, in the person of the father, is eager to welcome the son back and restore the relationship which has been broken.

SUMMARY
Christians believe that God is just. They believe that when someone does something wrong they should be offered forgiveness in order to help them reform and become what God wants them to become. God will ensure that justice is done.

38

A Beautiful World

God's handiwork

❑ Do you have a gift from someone which is very special to you? What makes it so special?

❑ How would you feel if someone destroyed or damaged this gift?

❑ Do you treat something you own differently from something which is on loan to you?

66 My children often bring things home from school which they have lovingly made—sculptures, pictures etc. One special gift which they gave me was a clay head. You can even see their fingerprints in it where they have touched the wet varnish. Each one of these gifts contains something of the child who gave it to me and reminds me of their particular personality and interests. I will always treasure them. 99

Margaret

The gifts these children had made bore something of their stamp. Christians believe that creation bears the stamp of God the Creator and that one way of knowing God is to look at his handiwork in the world.

66 If we look at the world around us we will learn something of God. We can glimpse something of his beauty in each flower. We can see his perfection in the extraordinary complexity of the design of the universe. We glimpse something of his awesome strength in the powerful forces of nature, in the wind, in earthquakes, volcanoes and the strength of the seas; and of his gentleness in the caressing breeze rustling through new leaves in spring. As we look into the stars and contemplate what lies beyond we glimpse the incomprehensible nature of the infinite. 99

Barbara Wood, *Our World, God's World*, The Bible Reading Fellowship

In his letter to the people in Rome, Paul writes:

Ever since God created the world, his invisible qualities have been clearly seen; they are perceived in the things that God has made.

Romans 1:20

World on loan

Who owns the world? Do kings and presidents, landowners or farmers? Christians believe that the world is a gift from God—it is on loan to people. The biblical story of creation says that 'the Lord God placed the man in the Garden of Eden to cultivate it and guard it.' (Genesis 2:15)

66 How we treat the world tells people something about our relationship to God. 99

Jessica, 16

BRAIN ENGAGE

1a Read the biblical account of the creation of the world. (Genesis 1—2:4) Make a diary account for each day using both words and pictures.

1b What do the following passages tell you about Christian attitudes to the world—Genesis 2:15; Psalm 8; Psalm 19:1?

2a What does Chief Seattle say about the earth? Make a list of five statements. How does his attitude to the earth differ from the White People's attitude? Pick out the statements in his speech which support the Christian belief about the world. Explain your choice.

2b Do you agree with Chief Seattle? Explain your answer.

2c If we had the same attitude to the world as Chief Seattle, how differently would we treat the world?

In 1854 Chief Seattle delivered the following speech to the American government who wanted to buy land from the Native Indians. As you read it, consider his attitude to the world.

66 How can you buy or sell the sky? How can you buy or sell the warmth of the land? This idea is strange to us. The freshness of the air and the sparkle of the water are not ours to sell, so how can anyone buy them? Every part of this earth is very, very special to my people. The perfumed flowers are our sisters. The deer, the horse, the great eagle, they are our brothers.

To a White Person, one piece of land is the same as another. White People take from the land what ever they need. The earth is not a brother, but an enemy. The White People's greed will destroy the earth and leave only a desert. Man did not weave the web of life; he is merely a strand in it. Whatever he does to the web, he does to himself... to harm the earth is to heap contempt on its creator.

This we know. The earth does not belong to us; we belong to the earth. All things are linked together. We are all part of one big family. 99

Adapted from *The Practical Assembly Guide* by A. Lovelace, Heinemann Educational

SUMMARY
••••••••••••
Christians believe that the world is God's world and that God loves the world. God has given it to us on loan. We are to be responsible managers of the world.

39

Endangered Earth

> 66 Planet Earth is 46 million years old. If we scale this down to 46 years then modern man has been around for four hours, and the Industrial Revolution began a minute ago. During those 60 seconds... man has multiplied his numbers to plague proportions, ransacked the planet for fuels and raw materials, and caused the extinction of countless species of animals and plants. 99

Jonathon Porritt, *Save the Earth*, Dorling Kindersley

Today the earth faces so many environmental dangers it could be described as being like a giant bomb waiting to explode. It would appear that we have not taken great care of the earth.

In 1987 the Brundtland Report on 'Our Common Future' brought the world's attention to the idea of 'sustainable development'. This means that we must take care with providing what we need on the earth without destroying the earth for future generations. Many people are thinking that we need to take a serious look at our lifestyles, especially in the west.

Our materialistic society encourages us to buy more goods and to seek greater wealth, indeed, advertisements tell us that happiness comes from the goods we buy. However, our level of consumption is having a costly effect on the planet... we use renewable resources unwisely; we over-fish the oceans, destroy the rain forest for short-term profit and throw away many resources that could easily be recycled.

Steps Towards Sustainability, Christian Ecology Link

Did you know?

ACID RAIN

🌢 Acid rain is caused mainly by sulphur dioxide and nitrogen oxides. Every year 115 million tonnes of sulphur dioxide and around 30 million tonnes of nitrogen oxides are released by the major industrialized nations.

🌢 Thousands of square miles of forest have been destroyed by acid rain all over the world.

Did you know?

GLOBAL WARMING

🌢 Most scientists agree that the smoke, carbon dioxide fumes and exhaust created by cars and factories are altering the world's climate. The pollution in the atmosphere traps heat like a greenhouse.

🌢 Destruction of the ozone layer leads to horrific increases in skin cancers, blindness and loss of food production.

BRAIN ENGAGE

1a Rose Elizabeth Bird, Chief Justice, California said, 'We have probed the earth, excavated it, burned it, ripped things from it, buried things in it... That does not fit my definition of a good tenant. If we were here on a month-to-month basis, we would have been evicted long ago.' Do you agree?

1b Christians believe that God is the 'landlord'. Imagine the letter God might write to people commenting on how he views them as tenants.

2a What would you do if you had political power? Suggest two ways in which you would lead a Green Revolution.

2b What would you do if you had God's power?

2c Design a SAVING THE WORLD poster.

Did you know?

POLLUTION AND WASTE

🔥 One fifth of the world's population is breathing air which is unsafe.

🔥 Our oceans are littered with plastic, sewage discharges, industrial wastes, farm pesticides and oil spills. In many parts of the world fish are found with tumours caused by pollutants.

🔥 In Britain enough aluminium cans are thrown away each year that, put end to end, they would reach to the moon and back.

Did you know?

DESTRUCTION OF RAIN FORESTS

🔥 An area of tropical rain forests four times the size of Switzerland disappears every year. *In Central America it is largely to provide pasture for cattle to feed the American hamburger market. In Australia and the Far East it is to fill the ever-hungry paper mills of Japan.* Poor countries such as Brazil are being encouraged to destroy their rain forests to gain money to pay their foreign debt.

🔥 *Tropical rain forests cover 7% of the land surface of the earth yet they contain 50% of the world's species.* If the forests vanish, so will more than 1 million species. The burning of the forests releases vast amounts of carbon dioxide into the atmosphere increasing the greenhouse effect.

Extracts in italics from *Our World, God's World* by Barbara Wood, The Bible Reading Fellowship

List the effects to the environment caused by this one industrial site.

SUMMARY
The earth is in danger of being destroyed by human hands. People must speak out and act if the planet is to be saved.

40

Battle to Save the Planet

Warnings

Until about fifty years ago, people thought that the earth had endless amounts of resources to keep the planet going. However, recently environmentalists have been trying to wake people up with the message 'Change your ways, or the world as you know it will be destroyed.' Scientists look at trends and predict serious trouble ahead if we continue to exploit the world.

The following environmental parable suggests reasons why the planet is in such a mess and raises the question of what people should do to save the planet.

There was this huge spaceship travelling through space at 66,000 miles an hour. There were many thousands of people on board all of whom had been born on the spaceship. The spaceship grew all its own food and contained all the water and air that were needed to keep life going on for ever.

The people on the spaceship were divided into two main groups: firstly, a small group of officers and their families who took control of the spaceship; secondly, the larger group of crew and their families, whose job it was to do all the hard labouring work.

For many years the spaceship seemed a fairly happy place, but as the years passed there were more and more problems. The ship's water was becoming dirty, its air was becoming poisoned, and the food-growing areas of the ship were being damaged due to the apparatus needed to provide more and more luxuries for the officers. There was a growing number of deaths among the crew's children because they were not getting enough to eat. Some of the officers' wives sent food parcels and some of the officers' children collected money and sent it down to the crew. But this help was not enough. Furthermore, there was a growing number of quarrels between the officers themselves and the officers and the crew.

'We'd better leave this spaceship,' said some of the people. 'It's terrible living here. Let's go away.' But there was nowhere else for them to go.

Adapted from *Moments of Reflection* by J. Howarth and M. Walton, Heinemann Educational

The sickness we see in our natural environment is the manifestation of a process of disregard and violence towards God's creation, something which the prophets of old called sin against God, sin against the work of his hands.

Barbara Wood, *Our World, God's World*, The Bible Reading Fellowship

Jesus commanded his disciples, 'Do not store up riches for yourselves here on earth.' (Matthew 6:19)

66 The western world is so caught up in making more and more money to buy more and more goods that they are robbing the earth of its resources. One author put it like this: 'We are celebrating our consumers' party on the edge of a volcano which could erupt any minute.' 99

Jeff

Christians, then, should seek to live simply so that others may simply live and that the earth might endure.

Steps Towards Sustainability, Christian Ecology Link

Could there be any grounds for justifying the deforestation and pollution shown in the photos?

Brain Engage

1a Make a 'simple living plan'. Imagine that you will have to live for a whole year on whatever you can pack into one small suitcase. You can only take things you already have! What will you take? What will you miss? In what ways will your lifestyle change?

1b In the light of your findings, write a brochure inviting people to adopt a simpler lifestyle. Model it on travel leaflets advising people what to take on a special holiday.

2a What do the spaceship, the officers and the crew stand for in the parable? What does this parable teach about (i) the relationships between officers and crew (ii) the reasons for problems arising on the ship (iii) possible solutions to the problems?

2b What Christian message does this parable teach about (i) the world as one family (ii) the inequality between people (iii) what people should do to save the planet?

3 Each year a day is set aside for people to stop and think what they are doing to the earth, and to warn people everywhere that the clock is ticking, and the hour is late. The first Earth Day was celebrated on 22 April 1970. People all over the world celebrate it in different ways. How would you celebrate Earth Day?

Summary

Christians believe that people should wake up to what is happening to the earth, to speak out against greed and exploitation of the earth and to think creatively of how they can use their money and resources to help poorer countries and therefore the earth.

● ●

❑ How should people treat animals?

❑ Do animals have any rights?

❑ Make a list of all the ways in which animals are badly treated—the photographs in this unit will help to start your thinking.

❝ Whilst I believe that animals should not be abused there is nothing wrong in eating them. ❞

Ann

❝ People should treat animals with respect. Animals have intelligence and can feel pain. ❞

John

❝ I am a vegetarian because I believe we have no right to kill animals. All life is sacred. ❞

Bella

Each day between 3 and 50 species of life become extinct. By AD2000, 15–20% of all species on earth may have disappeared due to human activities. That is, about 1,000,000 species will have become extinct.

The New Road, WWF Network

BRAIN ENGAGE

1 In groups write out your own list of animal rights. Present these in the form of a poster for the classroom wall.

2a Apply the biblical teaching to each of the photographs. What do you think the Christian position would be?

2b What reasons might a Christian give for being vegetarian? Should all Christians be vegetarian?

2c Many people are willing to buy a chicken from a supermarket but they wouldn't go out and kill the animal themselves. Discuss why.

3 Carry out your own research into one of the issues raised in these photographs. Write up your findings in the form of a fact sheet.

❑ Design your own postcard giving your views on animals.

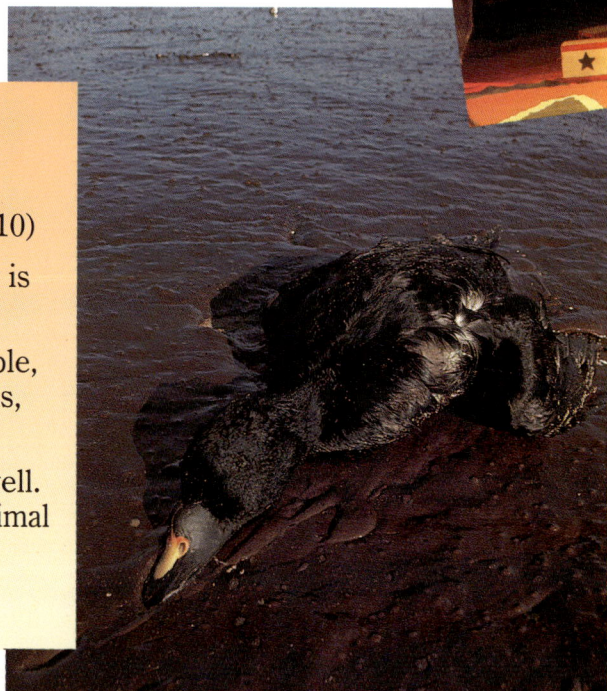

📁 BIBLE FILE

✠ 'A good man takes care of his animals, but wicked men are cruel to theirs.' (Proverbs 12:10)

✠ God cares for each animal; 'not one sparrow is forgotten by God.' (Luke 12:6)

✠ When God created the world he said to people, 'I am putting you in charge of the fish, the birds, and all the wild animals.' (Genesis 1:28)

✠ Biblical laws were careful to treat animals well. For example, the farmer should not stop an animal eating some of the crop whilst it was working. (Deuteronomy 25:4)

Discuss the following issues:

❏ Much of today's meat is produced by factory farming.

❏ An estimated 200 million animals are used for laboratory tests each year—some to test cosmetics and some to test drugs for medicines.

❏ Humans hunt animals for profit and fun. Some animals (e.g. whales, pandas, tigers) are becoming extinct due to hunting.

SUMMARY
Christians believe that people should be good stewards in the way they treat animals.

Where am I going?

Refugees are people who have no permanent home. They have been forced to leave their homes or their country, either because there is a war there or because of their political or religious beliefs. Today there are at least 19 million people who are forced to live as refugees outside their own countries.

The long journey

The Bible uses this image of refugees to talk about people's lives on earth. Christians believe that because humanity has turned its back on God, people have been forced to leave their real home with God. (Genesis 3:23) However, they believe that life does not end with death and that God promises they have a permanent home with him in the future. (John 14:1–2) This promise of a permanent home affects how Christians think about living and dying.

Many religions use the image of a journey to talk about life. The issue is how to spend the journey. The following quotation talks about this journey of life. What do you think it is trying to say?

On a long air flight passengers have to be distracted with frequent meals, films and music programmes, because they are 'on hold' for the duration of the flight. This is how a lot of people pass the time between birth and death—they live their life seeking pleasures and distractions, whether it be money, possessions or relationships. Some people go through all of their life without any real purpose or final meaning—all they do is distract themselves with the pleasures of life.

Adapted from *Crossfire* by Richard Holloway, HarperCollins Publishers Ltd

BIBLE FILE

✢ The Bible says we are 'strangers and refugees in this world'. (1 Peter 2:11)

✢ 'There is no permanent city for us here on earth; we are looking for the city which is to come.' (Hebrews 13:14)

✢ 'We are citizens of heaven.' (Philippians 3:20)

BRAIN ENGAGE

1a Make a list of things you would carry with you if you had to flee your home. Which would be the most important thing? Why?

1b In groups, brainstorm the feelings associated with being a refugee—what do you think it feels like to leave home and country?

1c Have any of you lived in a foreign country? What do you think the differences are living in a foreign country compared to living permanently in your home country?

2a Do you think Richard Holloway's view is an accurate way of describing how people spend their lives?

2b Draw a picture to illustrate this view. Give your picture a title.

3 Carry out a survey amongst your class to find out what people think happens after death. Write down what your own views are.

4 Beliefs about life affect how people behave in life. Here are three people's views:

◆ Susan believes that this life is all there is; this is her permanent home.

◆ Mike believes that this life is not all there is. His permanent home is with God.

◆ Ann is unsure what she believes. Sometimes she agrees with Susan and sometimes with Mike.

Get into groups of three. Choose a part to play, either Susan, Mike or Ann. Discuss how your viewpoint affects the way to live and treat things and people.

EXTRA

5 Prepare for a class debate on the motion 'This class believes that earth is not our permanent home.' Choose to support or oppose this statement and write your speech.

In units 42–44 we will be exploring issues to do with the future—our own futures and the world's future.

Home

In the following poem, Emily Dickinson (1830–1886) expresses her belief in this permanent home with God even though she has not yet seen it:

I never saw a moor
I never saw the sea;
Yet know I how the heather looks
And what a wave must be.

I never spoke with God,
Nor visited in Heaven;
Yet certain am I of the spot
As if the chart were given.

What tells you in this picture that these people have no permanent home?

SUMMARY

Christians believe that life is a journey with a purpose. Earth is not their permanent home. Instead, they are refugees here on earth. Their permanent home is with God in heaven.

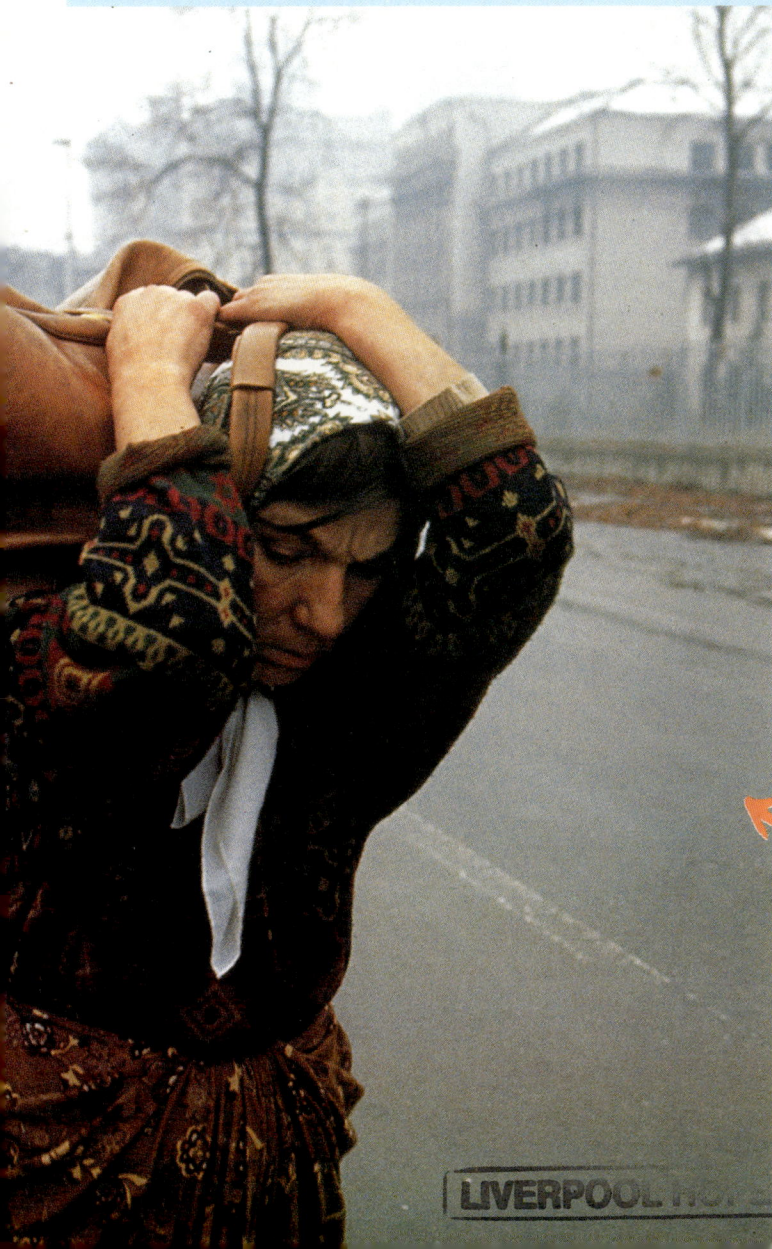

Today approximately 200,000 people died. Although death is such a common occurrence and the one thing of which we can all be certain, many people avoid talking about it.

❑ **Why do you think this is?**

❑ **Do you talk about death? Have you come close to death—e.g. have you seen a dead body? If so, what did you think and feel?**

❑ **Why do you think some people are frightened of death?**

Death reminds people that they cannot take anything with them to the grave—no money or people. Death therefore makes people wake up to the question of the purpose of life. Are we born just to die?

Lope de Vega was a great Spanish writer. Throughout his life he was admired—he had written over a thousand plays. To all outward appearances, his life was one huge success. However, as he lay on his deathbed, his life passed before him like a film and he suddenly saw things in a different light. The doctor who was with him said, 'You can die happy now knowing that you have been a great success and that the world will never forget you or your plays.' The dying man replied, 'I see it all now. Before God, only one with a good heart is great. How gladly would I now give all the praise I have had in my whole life if I could do one more good deed in exchange.'

Pierre Lefevre, *One Hundred Stories to Change Your Life*, St Pauls (UK)

❝ **Belief in life beyond death affects the way I see this life. Life on earth is a training for what lies ahead.** ❞

Chris

📁 BIBLE FILE

✦ Christians believe that life is a gift from God to be enjoyed. 'This is the day which the Lord has made; let us rejoice and be glad in it.' (Psalm 118:24) Some Christians speak of the sacrament of the present moment: the sacredness of each moment, seeking to do God's will in each moment of life.

✦ But Jesus warned his disciples that there was more to life than this world and its attractions: 'Will a person gain anything if he wins the whole world but loses his soul?' (Matthew 16:26)

✦ When Jesus was talking about his followers, he said, 'Just as I do not belong to the world, they do not belong to the world.' (John 17:16)

IT'S NOT THE PACE OF LIFE THAT CONCERNS ME.

IT'S THE SUDDEN STOP AT THE END. NO FEAR

BRAIN ENGAGE

1 Death has been described by different people in many ways. Which of the following views is closest to yours?

66 **Death is an enemy. It takes away from us all that we most love in life.** 99

Jean

66 **Death is a gateway or a brick wall depending on your view.** 99

A. Bullock

66 **Death is a comma, not a full stop.** 99

Ellen Wilkey

66 **Death is an exclamation mark emphasizing the importance of life.** 99

Kevin

66 **Welcome, Sister Death.** 99

St Francis

66 **Death is the terrible intruder.** 99

R. MacKenna

66 **Death is nothing but going home to God.** 99

Mother Teresa

2 M. Holmes described death as 'so utterly still... more still than the quietest meadow on a summer day. Stiller than the whitest snows of a winter hillside.' Draw your own picture to explain what you think about death. Think up your own description of death and use it as a title. What colours are you going to use to convey your image?

3 What do you think about the following opinion?

66 **It would be good if society could be more open about death... if we could start to take our children to funerals, for example.** 99

P. Yorkstone

4a Imagine that you are on your deathbed, looking back on your life so far. What, if anything, would you change?

4b Consider those things and think about how you could change them now.

66 **The centre of my faith is a relationship with a personal God who I can talk and listen to. If you've chatted with God all of your life you do get to know him as a friend and father. So I'm not frightened of death because I'm curious to meet at last the God whose voice I've talked to for so many years.** 99

Lionel

SUMMARY
• • • • • • • • • • • •
Christians believe that death is not the final frontier to be feared. Life in this world is a preparation for an eternity with God in heaven.

❏ **What sort of world do you think will exist in the future?**

Here is one 15-year-old's view of the world as she thinks it will exist on 14 August 2045.

14 August 2045

Consumer Relations Department
World Manufacturing Ltd.

Dear Sir/Madam,

With regard to your recent catalogue which describes your supplies for the next decade: I am sure that there will not be much need for the exhaust fumes and chemical-filled water you advertise on page nine. They are a bit cheaper than the clean air and water appearing on later pages, but much more unpleasant.

The wars you offer on pages 15-18 seem terribly unnecessary. I had hoped that you would not be repeating these offers from your last catalogue. However, I was not at all attracted by your two-for-the-price-of-one oil slick-and-war special bargain, and the family-sized world war is appalling. I intend to order your alternative peace contracts and help-the-refugees offers, even though the prices have not been lowered.

I see you have devoted thirty pages to crime, even some new varieties. I should congratulate your staff, but I don't think this sort of temptation is fair.

Your marketing campaign needs a little work, but I shall send in my order in a few days.

Yours faithfully,

A. Consumer

Imogen Goodyear, 15

The new Kingdom

Christians hope for a better world, a world which is restored. This hope is grounded in the nature of God as a king of justice who promises to right the wrongs in the world. Suffering, injustice and sin are against God's promises and therefore God will bring them to an end.

The Bible promises that Jesus will return to bring in a new heaven and a new earth. The prophet Micah put it in the following words:

He will settle disputes among the nations,
among the great powers near and far,
They will hammer their swords into ploughs
and their spears into
pruning-knives.
Nations will never
again go to war,
never prepare for
battle again.
Everyone will live in
peace among his own
vineyards and
fig-trees,
and no one will make him afraid.
The Lord Almighty has promised this.

Micah 4:3–4

The writer of the book of Revelation describes the new heaven and earth in the following way:

Then I saw a new heaven and a new earth... I heard a loud voice speaking from the throne: 'Now God's home is with mankind! He will live with them, and they shall be his people... He will wipe away all tears from their eyes. There

will be no more death, no more grief or crying or pain. The old things have disappeared.' Then the one who sits on the throne said, 'And now I make all things new!'

Revelation 21:1, 3–6

66 My heaven is not somewhere else. It is here but buried. Heaven is the Kingdom and the Kingdom has to be built. That means effort, not just hanging around. It means using whatever talents one has been given to try to build a community of people and a world that reflects, in part at least, the ideas of love and justice that God has put into our hearts. 99

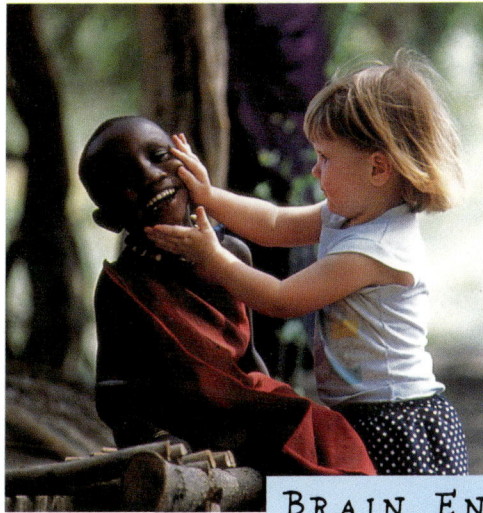

Bruce Kent, Vice-President of Campaign for Nuclear Disarmament

❏ **What is your hope for the future?**

BRAIN ENGAGE

3 What are the ingredients of the Christian hope for the future?

4 Write your own poem, or draw your own illustration to show 'What The World Needs' in order to bring about God's kingdom.

SUMMARY
• • • • • • • • • •
Christians believe that God is a king of justice who will right the world's wrongs at the end of time. Christians believe they are to work with God to bring about his kingdom on earth.

Text copyright © 1997 Chris Wright
This edition copyright © 1997 Lion Publishing
The author asserts the moral right
to be identified as the author of this work

Published by
Lion Publishing plc
Sandy Lane West, Oxford, England
ISBN 0 7459 3420 X
Lion Publishing
4050 Lee Vance View, Colorado Springs, CO 80918, USA
ISBN 0 7459 3420 X
Albatross Books Pty Ltd
PO Box 320, Sutherland, NSW 2232, Australia
ISBN 0 7324 1401 6

First edition 1997
10 9 8 7 6 5 4 3 2 1 0
All rights reserved
A catalogue record for this book is available
from the British Library

Printed and bound in Spain by Bookprint

Acknowledgments

We would like to thank all those who have given us permission to include quotations in this book, as indicated in the list below. Every effort has been made to trace and acknowledge copyright holders of all the quotations included. We apologize for any errors or omissions that may remain, and would ask those concerned to contact the publishers, who will ensure that full acknowledgment is made in the future.

Text

Page 2: *A World in Our Hands*, Tricycle Press, Peace Child International.

Page 14, 74: The Youth Bible, New Century Version, Copyright ©1991 by Word Publishing, Dallas, Texas 75234. Used by permission.

Page 15: *Assemblies for School Children's Church* by R H Lloyd, The Religious and Moral Education Press.

Page 15: *Lots of Love* by Nanette Newman

Page 22: *The Times Educational Supplement* 15 December 1995. © Times Supplements Limited, 1996.

Page 27: © 1994 Desmond Tutu. Extracted from *The Rainbow People of God* published by Bantam, a division of Transworld Publishers Ltd. All rights reserved.

Page 35: © Third Way 1996. From an interview published in *Third Way* in April 1996.

Page 46: Quotations from Clare Short and Rachel Garley, taken from *Issues 4* by John Foster, HarperCollins Publishers Ltd.

Page 50-51: 'True Love Waits' material © copyright 1994 Convention Press. All rights reserved. Used by permission.

Page 51: Jill Knight quoted in *Life in a Sex-Mad Society* by Joyce Huggett, IVP 1988.

Page 56: *Inside Stories* by Wood and Richardson, Trentham Books 1992.

Page 58, 88: *One Hundred Stories to Change Your Life* by Pierre Lefèvre. Reproduced by permission of St Pauls (UK).

Page 67: *Shadowlands* Copyright © by Universal City Studios, Inc. Courtesy of MCA Publishing Rights, a Division of MCA Inc. All rights reserved.

Page 69: *Celtic Fire* by Robert van de Weyer. Copyright ©1990 by Robert van de Weyer. Used by permission of Darton Longman & Todd Ltd and by permission of Doubleday, a division of Bantam Doubleday Dell Publishing Group, Inc.

Page 71: From *Faith and Struggle in Central America* Schools Pack published by CAFOD and Christian Aid.

Page 72: *Paradoxes of Christian Faith and Life* by Richard Holloway. Permission to reproduce extract granted by Mowbray, an imprint of Cassell plc.

Page 72: From *King's College Newsletter* December 1984. Permission given by Desmond Tutu.

Page 72 and 73: We would like to thank HarperCollins publishers for permission to quote from Collins Cobuild English Dictionary, 1995.

Page 74: 'Statistics suggest... sugar and salt' from *Christianity In Today's World* by Jenkins and Smith. Extract reproduced with the permission of BBC Worldwide Limited.

Page 75: *Meet Christ And Live* by Michel Quoist, Gill and Macmillan 1973.

Page 77: Dr Paul Oestreicher, Letter to Editor, The Times 22.1.96.

Page 79: *The Practical Assembly Guide* by A Lovelace; reprinted by permission of Heinemann Educational, a division of Reed Educational and Professional Publishing Ltd.

Page 80: By permission of Jonathon Porritt.

Page 80, 82: From *Steps Towards Sustainability* Resource Pack published 1994 by Christian Ecology Link, Carlton Road, Harrogate HG2 8DD.

Page 82: *Moments of Reflection* by J Howarth and M Walton; reprinted by permission of Heinemann Educational, a division of Reed Educational and Professional Publishing Ltd.

Page 86: *Crossfire* by Richard Holloway, HarperCollins Publishers Ltd.

Page 90: Bruce Kent, Vice President of Campaign for Nuclear Disarmament, quoted in *I will see you in heaven* by Michael Seed. Reproduced by permission of St Pauls (UK).

Photographs

COVER
Susanna Burton: (above right, centre right, below right)

Environmental Images: (centre left)

Zefa Pictures: (above far left, above left, below left, below centre)

INSIDES
Susanna Burton: pages 20 (below right), 38 (centre left, below right), 57 (above left), 91 (above centre)

Christian Aid/CAFOD: page 69 (centre)

Meryl Doney: page 40 (centre left)

© Ecoscene: /Anthony Cooper page 5 (right); /Gryniewicz page 82 (below right); /Hulme page 85 (centre right); /Chris Knapton page 81 (above left); /Lees page 90 (centre right); /Rob Nichol page 84 (below centre)

Sonia Halliday Photographs: page 9 (above centre)

Leprosy Mission: page 25 (centre right)

Lion Publishing: 23 (above), 33 (above right), 60 (centre), 61 (above left), 79 (above left); /Nigel Poulton page 75 (below left); /David Townsend pages 3 (centre right), 24 (above right), 30 (above left), 52 (right), 72 (centre left), 73 (below centre), 78/79 (below centre), 85 (above right)

Musée d'Orsay, Paris/Bridgeman Art Library, London (Credit Lauros Giraudon/Bridgeman Art Library): page 11 (below right)

Panos Pictures: /Sami Sallinen page 70 (above right)

Photo Oikoumene/World Council of Churches: pages 27 (above centre), 82/83 (whole spread); /Wolf Kutnahorsky pages 80/81 (below centre); /Rick Reinhard page 72 (above centre); /Peter Williams pages 26/27 (centre), 68 (below), 70/71 (below centre)

Photofusion: /Paul Baldesare page 10 (below left); /Tim Dub page 38 (above right); /Hannah Gal page 37 (centre right); /Gina Glover page 35 (below left); /Crispin Hughes page 70 (above left); /Paul Mattsson page 47 (below centre); /George Montgomery page 34 (above right); /Gary Parker page 32 (below left, below right); /Christa Stadtler page 74 (above right)

Rex Features Ltd: pages 67 (centre left), 72 (above right); /Peter Brooker page 63 (above right); /Tom Haley pages 86/87 (below centre); /David Henley page 4 (left); /Craig Johnson pages 28/29 (centre); /Pierrot Leloup page 8 (above left); /Leon Schadeberg page 53 (above right); /Shone pages 62/63 (below centre)

Nicholas Rous: pages 8 (below left), 29 (centre right), 66 (below centre)

Società Scala, Florence: pages 14/15 (below centre), 31 (below centre)

Science Photo Library/Nestle/Petit Format: page 54 (below)

David Simson: pages 18/19 (centre), 24 (below centre), 57 (above right)

Skjold Photographs: pages 6 (below centre), 12 (centre left), 20 (above right), 26 (above left), 55 (below right), 58 (below right)

Staatliche Kunsthalle, Karlsruhe/Bridgeman Art Library, London: page 64 (centre right)

Still Pictures: /Mike Schroder page 24 (centre left)

SuperStock Ltd: pages 16 (right), 45 (below right), 77 (centre left)

Tate Gallery Publishing: pages 6/7 (centre)

John Williams Studios: pages 10 (centre), 14 (centre left, centre right), 23 (above left), 36 (above centre, centre right), 37 (centre left), 42 (centre left), 44 (above right, below right), 51 (above right), 56 (above centre), 65 (centre), 78 (above left), 81 (below right), 86 (below left)

Chris Wright: page 88 (below left)

Zefa Pictures: pages 1 (below centre), 12 (above right), 13 (centre), 19 (above right), 30 (below centre), 32 (above left, centre right, above right), 34 (above left, above centre), 41 (above right), 46 (centre right, above right), 48 (centre), 50/51 (below centre), 67 (above), 85 (below centre, centre left), 89 (centre left, centre right), 91 (below)

Illustrations

Beehive Illustration: pages 42 (centre right), 43 (centre left, centre right, below left), 76 (above left, centre left)

Useful Addresses

Many of these organizations are registered charities and rely on donations to survive. It is therefore important that you clearly state what information you require and send a stamped addressed envelope with your request for information.

Action by Christians Against Torture
32 Wentworth Hills
Wembley
Middlesex
HA9 9SG

Amnesty International
99-119 Rosebery Avenue
London
EC1R 4RE
Tel: 0171 814 6200

Animal Aid
The Old Chapel
Bradford Street
Tonbridge
Kent
TN9 1AW
Tel: 01732 364546

CAFOD
2 Romero Close
Stockwell Road
London
SW9 9TY
Tel: 0171 733 7900

Catholic Truth Society
192 Vauxhall Bridge Road
London
SW1V 1PD
Tel: 0171 834 4392

Childline
Tel: 0800 1111

Christian Aid
PO Box 100
London
SE1 7RT
Tel: 0171 620 4444

Church of England Enquiries Centre
Church House
Great Smith Street
London
SW1P 3NZ
Tel: 0171 222 9011

Commission for Racial Equality
Elliot House
10-12 Allington Street
London
SW1E 5EH
Tel: 0171 828 7022

El Salvador Committee for Human Rights
83 Margaret Street
London
W1N 7HB

EXIT (Voluntary Euthanasia Society)
13 Prince of Wales Terrace
London
W8 5PG
Tel: 0171 937 7770

Friends of the Earth
26-28 Underwood Street
London
N1 7JQ
Tel: 0171 490 1555

Gay Christian Movement
BM 6914
London
WC1N 3XX

Greenpeace
Canonbury Villas
London
N1 2PN
Tel: 0171 865 8100

LIFE
Life House
Newbould Terrace
Leamington Spa
Warwickshire
CV32 4EH
Tel: 01926 311511

National Abortion Campaign
The Print House
18 Ashwin Street
London
E8 3DL
Tel: 0171 923 4976

Oxfam
274 Banbury Road
Oxford
OX2 7DZ
Tel: 01865 311311

Refugee Council
3 Bond Way
London
SW8 1SJ
Tel: 0171 820 3000

Salvation Army Headquarters
101 Queen Victoria Street
London
EC4P 4EP
Tel: 0171 236 5222

Samaritans
10 The Grove
Slough
Berks
SL1 1QP
Tel: 01753 532713

Tear Fund
100 Church Road
Teddington
Middlesex
TW11 8QE
Tel: 0181 977 9144

Worldwide Fund for Nature
Panda House
Weyside Park
Godalming
Surrey
GU7 1XR
Tel: 01483 426444

Index

a

abortion 30, 54, 55

Abortion Rights Action League 55

abuse 37, 40, 41, 84

acid rain 80

Adam 10, 11, 73

addiction 14, 15, 36, 37, 65

adolescence 32, 33, 37, 48, 51

adultery 50, 60, 77

AIDS 51, 61

alcohol 14, 36, 37, 65

anger 45

ambassador 26, 27

animals 2, 84, 85

anorexia 36

apartheid 27, 72

b

bitterness 23

body 34, 36, 37, 46

c

choices 15, 20, 29, 55, 62, 65

commitment 52, 53

conception 54, 55

conflict 32, 33, 42, 60

creation 10, 30, 31, 36, 62, 65, 78, 79, 82

d

David (King) 12, 51, 64

death 17, 44, 60, 61, 67, 86, 87, 88, 89

deforestation 82

destruction 28, 81

Devil 28, 29, 45, 62, 63

discipline 38, 39

discrimination 72, 73

disobedience 55

divorce 40

drugs 25, 36, 37, 43, 65, 85

duty 39, 41

e

Ecstasy 37

education 2

enemies 24, 25, 44, 53, 64

environment 80, 81, 82

euthanasia 30

Eve 10, 11, 73

evil 25, 60, 62, 63, 77

f

faith 18, 19, 26, 67

family 38, 39, 40, 75, 79

forgiveness 14, 21, 22, 23, 27, 39, 49, 50, 51, 55, 63, 71, 76, 77

free will 62, 65

friendship 6, 17, 32, 34, 42, 43, 51

future 86, 90

g

GOD'S CHARACTERISTICS 8, 30, 39
  God's image 31, 46, 71, 73
  God's Kingdom 6, 7, 29, 70, 90, 91
  God's love 27, 39, 40, 41, 65
  God's standards 5, 9, 14

Godzone 6, 7

Gomez, Maria Cristina 69

Good Samaritan 74

goodness 21

gossip 58

greed 71, 83

h

holiness 8, 21

Holy Spirit 21, 34, 36

homosexuality 47, 62

honesty 42, 49, 53

Hosea 9, 40

human rights 71

humility 21

hunger 2

hunting 85

i

injustice 23, 27, 68, 69, 70, 71, 77, 90, 91

Isaiah 8, 20, 21

j

Jesus 17, 19, 22, 24, 25, 26, 38, 39, 40, 44, 45, 48, 49, 60, 64, 65, 71, 74, 76, 77, 82

k

kindness 21, 25, 49, 53

knowledge 21, 52, 53

l

Lazarus 57

Lewis, C.S. 21, 67

liberation theology 70

lies 43, 59

LIFE 55

loss 12, 13

lostness 12, 13, 17, 29

love 6, 7, 8, 17, 21, 24, 25, 39, 42, 45, 47, 48, 51, 52, 53, 59, 71, 74, 76, 91

loyalty 42, 43, 49, 50

m

marriage 48, 50, 51, 52

maze 14

Medrach 19

money 56, 57